D1029826

THE

TEXAS RANGERS

Men of Valor and Action

By Mike Cox

EAKIN PRESS ★ **Austin, Texas**

Library of Congress Cataloging-in-Publication Data

Cox, Mike.
     The Texas Rangers : men of valor and action / by Mike Cox.
          p.   cm.
     Summary: True stories from the history of the Texas Rangers, who have
been looking out for the protection of Texans since 1823.
     ISBN 0-89015-818-5
     1. Texas Rangers — History — Juvenile literature. 2. Texas Rangers —
Biography — Juvenile literature. 3. Frontier and pioneer life — Texas —
Juvenile literature. 4. Texas — History — 1846–1950 — Juvenile literature. [1. Texas Rangers — History. 2. Texas Rangers — Biography.
3. Frontier and pioneer life — Texas. 4. Texas — History — 1846–1950.]
I. Title.
F391.C68   1991
976.4--dc20   91-16660
                                                                      CIP
                                                                      AC

For my mother,
Betty Wilke Hudman,
who got me started on the trail

And to my wife, Linda,
who helped me find
my inner child.

Books by Mike Cox

Red Rooster Country
"My Only Lasting Words"
Fred Gipson: Texas Storyteller
Lure of the Land (with Joe Frantz)
The Confessions of Henry Lee Lucas

Contents

Preface		vii
1.	"Rangers for the Common Defense"	1
2.	Capt. Jack Hays: "Bravo Too Much"	14
3.	"Rest In Peace" Ford	24
4.	The Frontier Battalion	33
5.	McNelly's Rangers	44
6.	The Lone Star Ranger: Capt. John R. Hughes	54
7.	Trailing *Tequileros*	67
8.	"I'm Frank Hamer"	81
9.	One-armed Bandits	95
10.	The Missing Dinosaur Tracks	105
Glossary		121
More Books About the Texas Rangers		125

Preface

My late grandfather, L. A. Wilke, liked to tell stories. He was good at it, though as he got older he tended to repeat himself a lot. I guess that was good, because I know some of his stories so well you'd think they were mine, not his. Today, with a two-year-old granddaughter of my own, I'm looking forward to sharing some of these stories with another generation.

Granddad particularly liked to talk about the Texas Rangers. As a reporter or editor for newspapers in San Antonio, Corpus Christi, Fort Worth, and El Paso during the 1920s and '30s, Granddad got to meet some of the Rangers who became legends in their own time. Men like Frank Hamer, Tom Hickman, Manuel T. "Lone Wolf" Gonzaullas, and John R. Hughes. He became friends with these tough lawmen, particularly with Hickman and Hughes.

Granddad had a story or two each about these old Rangers and others. He'd clear his throat and start off into a story while leaning back in his chair and tapping the armrest as he recalled the old days.

Maybe because he had spent so many years writing or editing newspaper stories, he seemed to think he couldn't get off into a story without first spelling the name of the person he was getting ready to talk about.

"I took a trip down into the Big Bend with a one-armed Ranger named Arch Miller, that's M-i-l-l-e-r," he might begin.

In 1927, when Granddad was city editor of the old

Fort Worth Press, a Scripps-Howard newspaper that finally went out of business in the mid-1970s, he covered what he called "The Battle of Borger."

Borger was a booming oil town in the Panhandle, and the city got so rough the governor decided to send in the Texas Rangers and the National Guard to settle folks down. Granddad rode on the train from Fort Worth to Borger with the Rangers, including Frank Hamer. A few years later, Hamer would gain international fame for killing the outlaw couple Bonnie and Clyde, but he already had a reputation as a very effective Ranger. He was fast and deadly with a .45.

Back in the 1920s, newspapermen sometimes carried pistols for self-protection. Knowing he was going to a town with no regard for law and order, Granddad had a small .25-caliber semi-automatic tucked inside his suit vest when he got on the train for Borger.

Hamer, with an instinct that helped him survive many gun battles, could tell when a man was carrying a pistol. He realized Granddad was armed. When Granddad dozed off in his train seat, Hamer expertly lifted the pistol from his pocket.

"You better not ever shoot me with this and let me find out about it," he laughed, and gave Granddad his gun back.

Of course, Granddad never shot anyone with that gun or any other. But he loved to tell the story. A few years later, Granddad was with Hamer when the big Ranger tried to hold off a lynch-minded mob outside the Grayson County Courthouse in Sherman.

Granddad saw the Rangers as men of valor and action. The Rangers helped build Texas by protecting its citizens from Indians, Mexican bandits, and outlaws. They did that by being tough. Sometimes, at least judged by our standards today, they were too tough. As Granddad grew older, and as crime in Texas and the nation seemed to become more common and more violent, he said the old Rangers he had known could straighten

Texas out again.

But those old Rangers were all gone, and so were the days when lawmen could slap a liar, pistol whip someone who didn't need killing, or shoot first and ask questions later.

Granddad's stories greatly influenced my interest in the Texas Rangers. I followed in his footsteps and became a newspaper writer myself. As a reporter, I also got to know some Texas Rangers. But I never dreamed as a young boy, or even as a young man, that someday I'd become the public information officer for the Texas Department of Public Safety, which includes the Texas Rangers.

Now I work with the Rangers on a daily basis and count many of them as my friends. I'll have some good stories to tell my grandchildren about today's Texas Rangers.

In this book, I've tried to show the history of the Texas Rangers in ten action stories. These stories are all based on true incidents from the annals of the Rangers. The retired Ranger in the story about gambling in Galveston and the Ranger in the story about the dinosaur track thief are composite characters, but all the other Rangers in the book were real. Dialogue has been added to make these stories interesting to read, but I am satisfied it has the ring of authenticity and that anything in this book that didn't happen at least could have happened.

Granddad did not live to see me write this book, but two other people in my life played important roles in its development.

My mother, Betty Wilke Hudman, Granddad's daughter, is a librarian who helped a lot with the research for this book. She also used to be an English teacher. When I don't know if a comma should be in a certain sentence, or where an apostrophe should be, or if my subject agrees with my verb, she's the person I call for help.

My wife, Linda Aronovsky Cox, who has her master's in communication, read this book and offered suggestions on how I could write it so children will both enjoy it and learn something from it. Often, on long walks, we would talk about the book and she'd encourage me as I fretted about one thing and then another concerning the writing of it. She also compiled the glossary at the end of the book.

Finally, I hope the young people I wrote this book for enjoy reading it as much as I enjoyed writing about the Texas Rangers.

1

"Rangers for the Common Defense"

Like almost everything else on the early frontier, paper was hard to come by and was seldom wasted. When Stephen F. Austin established the Texas Rangers, he used the back of a land colonization proclamation to officially record the act.

Stephen Fuller Austin was the man who brought the first Anglo-American settlers in 1821 to the land that would soon be called "Texas." Austin was an *empresario*.

Texas had come under the Mexican flag in 1821 and was legally a province of Mexico. Texans therefore were governed by Mexican laws. The governor of the Mexican province of Coahuila y Texas authorized a small company of mounted men to protect Austin's new colony against hostile Indians.

But Austin felt more men were needed and decided to strengthen the company at his own expense. The men would be paid $15 a month, not in money but in land — the only thing of value Austin could offer. The men had to furnish for themselves everything they needed to do the job.

So on August 5, 1823, Austin dipped the nib of his quill pen into his ink well and turned over a piece of paper that had a proclamation written on it by land commissioner Baron de Bastrop. He began to write on the back:

> I therefore by these presents give public notice that I will employ ten men in addition to those employed by the Government to act as rangers for the common defense.

Austin's 1823 announcement was the first known written use of the word "ranger" in Texas, though it was far from a new word. Its use dated back to earlier days in England. The term crossed the Atlantic with the colonials. Rangers played an important part in the French and Indian wars and in the American Revolution. The word was moving west with the frontier.

Austin clearly had the vision to realize it was a good idea to use local civilians in addition to more traditional military forces to protect settlers against Indians. But that was already happening unofficially when he wrote his public notice.

Civilians who came up with their own arms, horses, and food — and who rode when and where they were needed — were already protecting their own families against Indians and outlaws in Texas. But until Austin scratched out his defense plan, no one had gotten around to calling them rangers.

A few months earlier, in May 1823, Mexican governor Jose Felix Trespalacios had authorized ten men under Lt. Moses Morrison to protect settlers along the two longest streams in Texas, the Colorado and Brazos rivers. The men Austin hired rode with Morrison. They were involved in several fights with Indians and with outlaws of both Hispanic and Anglo heritage.

During their brief service, the Rangers under Lieutenant Morrison lost only one man, John Tumlinson. He was the first Texas Ranger to die in the line of duty. The well-liked frontiersman was killed by an Indian after offering his hand in friendship. Though Tumlinson made the ultimate sacrifice, his fellow Rangers apparently were never paid for their services.

By 1835, the Anglo population of Texas had swelled to more than 30,000 and there was growing unrest among the settlers with Mexican rule. That October, a group of men representing the various settlements in Texas passed a resolution creating a "Corps of Rangers" to protect the settlers from Indians.

In late November, a law creating a provisional, or temporary, government set the strength of the Rangers at 150 men. They were led by a major who reported to the government's military commander. This came as Texas moved toward declaring independence from Mexico and was the beginning of the Texas Rangers as a government service.

By 1836, the year the Republic of Texas came into being, "mounted riflemen" in "ranging service on the frontier" were paid $25 a month, plus free land. Officers, usually chosen by election, were paid $75 a month. Since the men had to furnish their own guns and horses, the money was barely enough to get by on.

One of three men selected as Ranger captains was John J. Tumlinson, the son of that first Ranger who gave his life for Texas. Captain Tumlinson's company saw plenty of action on the Western frontier of Texas.

*　　*　　*　　*　　*

Old Jennifer had been missing since dawn.

Sixteen-year-old Jason Harrell pushed through the cedar, listening for the familiar tinkle of the copper bell around their milch cow's neck. The January sky had turned the color of cold campfire ash and the wind was blowing from the north. Jason knew it would be much colder by nightfall.

Jennifer had never ventured this far before. Jason's

mother had gone out that morning to milk the cow and came back to the cabin crying.

"Jennifer's gone," Susana Harrell had sobbed. "I expect she's wandered off and got sick or some wildcat's eaten her. What are we going to do for milk?"

William Harrell tried to comfort his wife.

"Now, Mama, a panther's not going to jump a milch cow," he told her. "Them lions have all the deer they can say grace over." He cocked his head as though thinking. "Bear might of got her, though."

He had meant to get a laugh out of his worried wife, but mentioning a bear had not made Mrs. Harrell feel any better at all.

Finally, he handed Jason his flintlock rifle, the one he'd carried when the Texans ran the Mexican army out of San Antonio the year before.

"I've got some chores to do here," he told his son. "You work your way upriver and see if you can find that cow. While you're at it, may as well bring us back some meat. Bucks are going crazy after them doe now it's turned off cold. They're not thinking straight. You might get a dead shot."

Jason gripped the heavy Kentucky rifle, almost as long as he was tall, as he made his way up the Colorado River. Only two cabins, Reuben Hornsby's and old man William Barton's, were any farther upriver. Beyond Barton's place, beyond the cedar-covered hills to the west, were only buffalo and Indians.

Something gave a startled snort in the cedar trees. Jason saw a flash of white tail as a deer crashed through the brush. The sun was getting low and the deer were beginning to move, frisky and in rut.

Jason headed up a bluff to get a better view. A cedar branch slapped him in the face about the time he saw the big deer.

The buck stood frozen on the other side of the creek, staring at Jason as he tried to sort out the source of the danger he sensed.

4

The click the hammer made going back was as loud as thunder in Jason's ears, but the deer stood his ground.

Slowly, careful not to move too fast, Jason raised the heavy rifle and squinted down its long barrel. He lined up the sights right behind the buck's shoulder.

His papa had taught him to squeeze the trigger, which was just what he was starting to do when he heard the first awful bellow behind him. The buck dipped its antlers, wheeled, and disappeared in the brush.

Jason heard the familiar tinkle of Jennifer's bell. Swinging around with the rifle still on his shoulder, Jason was mad enough to shoot the old cow square between her eyes. Slowly, he lowered the rifle.

"Jennifer, you just scared off my buck, you old fool! Where the devil have you . . ."

Jason did not finish his question. Two arrows bristled from her blood-soaked neck.

$$* \quad * \quad * \quad * \quad *$$

Jennifer pitched and bellowed all the way back to the cabin.

Mrs. Harrell, burying her face in her apron, sank to her knees at the sight of the bloody cow and broke into tears.

"Oh, Lord, they've gone and killed Jennifer. Why would they shoot our poor old cow full of arrows? We're all going to be killed in this Godforsaken Texas."

Mr. Harrell put his arms around his wife. "I expect they didn't need the meat and figured to kill her out of pure meanness," he said. "Indians don't always do what we figure they will. Seabren Hamm tells the story of some Indians tossing a skunk inside their cabin. They did it just for spite, he reckoned. Comanches could have killed them all, but they didn't. Seabren heard 'em laughing as they rode off."

The story did not comfort Mrs. Harrell, who stared blankly at the wounded cow.

"Jennifer's still up, which is a blessing," Mr. Harrell

said. "If she don't take down with a fever after I get them arrows out, she'll live. I figure she's more scared than hurt. Come on, son, lend a hand."

Mrs. Harrell wiped away her tears with her apron. "I'll fix a poultice for the wounds," she said.

* * * * *

William Harrell sat just inside the cabin door all night, sound asleep, with the flintlock in his hands. The sound of riders woke him up. He pulled back the hammer of his rifle and peered out a crack in the door.

"Hello the house," one of the riders cried. "I'm Captain Tumlinson. You folks doing all right? There's Comanches hereabouts."

Mr. Harrell unlatched the door and stepped outside the cabin. Jason, rubbing the sleep from his eyes, was right behind his father. Mrs. Harrell, still in her nightgown, stayed inside.

The false dawn made it light enough for Jason to make out the roughest-looking group of riders he had ever seen. Some wore buckskin, others frock coats, but each carried a rifle, a brace of pistols, and wide-bladed Bowie knives. They were Rangers, the toughest fighters in Texas.

A man his father seemed to know got off his horse.

"Captain Tumlinson, how are you?" Mr. Harrell asked. "You are right about the Indians. They put two arrows in my milch cow. My boy Jason found her last night, still alive."

The captain shook his head.

"I've been commissioned to raise a company of sixty men. We're meeting up with the other boys at Hornsby's station, but I wanted to call on you before we reached there. We camped cold last night downriver a piece."

William Harrell leaned his rifle against the cabin.

"I expect you boys would appreciate some coffee, and I know Mrs. Harrell wouldn't want you to ride off without some bacon and biscuits."

"Well, we'd be mighty obliged," Captain Tumlinson replied. "I don't believe there will be much prospect for good victuals with Indians on the prowl."

The men ate like they had not had anything in their stomachs for a good while. Their enjoyment of her cooking was the first thing that had cheered Mrs. Harrell any since the wounding of Jennifer.

Before the Rangers settled down to get a few hours sleep, William Harrell saw his son talking with Captain Tumlinson. He had a good idea what it was about.

* * * * *

"Pa, Captain Tumlinson said I could saddle up with them this evening after they've rested up. I aim to go."

William Harrell did not have time to say anything before his wife spoke.

"Jason, you're too young to ride with the Rangers. You saw what those Indians did to Jennifer. Let the grown men go after them."

"Ma, I am nearly grown. I can ride and I can shoot. I would have carried us back a nice buck if it hadn't been for that old cow and them Indians. That's cause enough to ride after 'em."

But Jason knew it did no good to argue with his mother. He had just turned sixteen, but even if he were eighteen, she still would not want him to go. He would not mention it again, but as soon as she and his father were asleep that night, he would be leaving.

* * * * *

A full moon as big as an ox-cart wheel hung over the river.

Jason slipped out of the cabin and moved quietly toward the corral. Job, their gray gelding, whinnied in greeting as Jason went to the shed for the saddle.

When Jason stepped back out into the moonlight, the shadow of a big man loomed over him. Jason gasped before he realized it was his father.

7

"Son, your mother told you that you couldn't ride with the Rangers."

"I know, Pa, but . . ."

"Git, boy. You don't have to tell me how you're feeling. If it weren't for my back and that lead ball I took in San Antonio, I'd ride off with you. Go meet up with the captain. I imagine he'll be expecting you. I'll square it with your mama."

William Harrell handed his son the rifle. "I reckon you'll be needing this."

*   *   *   *   *

Jason reached Hornsby's station that afternoon. The Rangers had made camp outside Hornsby's cabin. Most of the Rangers squatted around a fire, their backs to the north wind. A blackened coffee pot sat in the coals. A hunk of meat hung over the oak fire, seasoning in the smoke.

Captain Tumlinson walked up as Jason swung out of his saddle.

"Well, son, you've had yourself a pretty fair ride up the river. Get that saddle off your horse. Then have yourself some meat. Our cooking may not be as good as your mama's, but help yourself."

Yesterday's norther was still blowing hard. Steam rose from his horse's sweaty skin when Jason pulled off Job's saddle. *By God, I'm making camp with the Rangers,* Jason thought to himself. Even though he had his father's blessing to leave home, he was sure glad the captain had not asked any questions. He did not want the men to know his mother still considered him a boy.

A jaunty man in buckskin walked up to Jason with a fair-sized hunk of juicy venison sticking on the end of his Bowie knife.

"Name's Smithwick," he said. "Have a piece of backstrap. Sorry I don't have anything to go with it. That was a mighty fine meal your mama cooked us yesterday. It lasted clear up 'til now."

Jason pulled the meat off the knife blade.

"I'm obliged," he said as he took a big bite of the hot meat, swallowed it nearly whole, and took another.

"Take your time, son," the older man said. "You look a might too excited. There ain't no particular glory in dodging Indian arrows, which is what I expect we'll end up doing before too long."

A shrill scream broke Jason's concentration on the venison.

*   *   *   *   *

A pretty young woman had emerged from the cedar and collapsed in exhaustion at the edge of the Ranger camp. Her torn dress barely clung to her bloody, mud-caked body. She whimpered like a small child.

Captain Tumlinson picked her up and carried her in both arms to the campfire, ordering a Ranger to fetch a blanket. "Pour this lady some coffee," he told the Ranger closest to the fire.

The captain bid his time before asking any questions.

"What happened to you, ma'am?" he finally asked.

She shook so badly she had to hold her coffee with both hands to keep it from sloshing out.

"I am Mrs. Hibbons," she began, fighting to control her voice. "The Indians . . . killed my baby. My husband. My brother."

Sobs overcame her. The captain waited, his jaws tight.

"We were on our way to our cabin on the Guadalupe when Comanches overtook us. After they finished with . . . with my husband, they took me and my baby and little boy with them. They tied me to one of their mules with my baby in my arms. My son was tied to another mule by himself."

The Rangers listened on grimly.

"When my littlest would not stop crying, one of

9

them snatched her from me and dashed her head against a tree . . ."

Again, the woman broke into uncontrollable sobbing.

After a few moments, she pulled the blanket tighter around herself and resumed her story.

"When this norther started blowing, the Indians lay up in a cedar brake. They must not have thought I'd try to get away with my child, so they didn't even tie me. They wrapped up in their buffalo robes and went to sleep.

"I knew I had to get away," she said, taking another sip of the coffee. "In another day's ride we would be too far beyond the settlements for hope. When I was satisfied they were deep in sleep, I wrapped a robe around my boy, kissed him goodbye, and slipped away. I died a little when I left him behind, but I knew he would make too much noise if I woke him and tried to take him with me.

"We had crossed the Colorado after my capture, and I knew there were cabins along the river, so I began following it downstream. I walked in the water as much as I could to cover my tracks.

"Once, I thought I heard my boy scream. I was certain the Indians would awaken, find that I had gone, and come after me. But the only sound I heard was the wind.

"I walked all morning and into the afternoon. I knew I was near help when I came up on a herd of cows, but I dared not call out for fear the Indians were following me. I hid in the brush until the cows were through grazing and started walking home. I followed them here. Now, please, go find my son before it's too late."

Captain Tumlinson ordered his men to finish their supper as fast as they could and then saddle up. Hornsby agreed to serve as guide.

They rode hard, well into the night. Jason fought sleep. He had not had any rest since slipping out of the cabin late the night before.

Finally, the captain called a halt.

"Boys, I'm worried that if we ride longer, we may

10

cross their trail and miss it. Let's get what rest we can and move out at first light."

But it was still dark when Smithwick nudged Jason. "Get up, son. Day's a wastin'."

Jason was glad he was too young to have a taste for coffee. Some of the older Rangers were carrying on like they could not lift their saddles without a cup of the dark brew first.

Hornsby was already gone, out looking for the trail.

The search was not long. Soon he rode back into camp.

"I've found their trail and it's fresh," he told the captain. "They're just lolly-gagging along like they've got all the time in creation. Guess they reckon nobody's fool enough to come after them."

Captain Tumlinson fairly leaped up on his saddle. "Let's go get that little boy."

The Rangers did not have a long trail to follow. The Indians had been overconfident.

"Lookit there," Smithwick whispered. "It'll be noon in a couple of hours and they're just now breaking camp."

Jason gripped his father's rifle tightly. He had killed deer and other animals, but he had never pointed the muzzle-loader at a man. He wondered what it would be like to have someone aim at him.

Captain Tumlinson did not leave him much time for reflection. "Charge 'em, boys," he yelled, spurring his horse.

The excitement was too much for Jason's horse Job, who seemed to think the Ranger charge was some kind of a race. The gelding pulled ahead of the other Rangers' horses and galloped straight into the Indian camp. All of a sudden, Jason was surrounded by Indians.

Jason saw the Indian pointing the musket in his direction and ducked his head behind Job's thick neck. The shot missed, but he heard it buzz by.

Job was too frenzied to control. Leaping off the wide-eyed gelding, Jason ran after the Indian who had shot at him. The Comanche had not had time to reload.

Jason stopped and fired. When he stepped away from the puff of blackpowder smoke left by the rifle, he saw the Indian lying motionless on the ground.

Yells and shots surrounded him. Reloading as he ran, Jason headed back into the thick of it — straight into a tree. The blow knocked his hat off and sent him crumpling to his knees.

Slowly, he got up and leaned against the tree. As he stooped to pick up his hat, Jason saw that the Indian he had hit was not dead. The Comanche had reloaded and was pointing his rifle toward the captain.

With a terrifying scream, the captain's horse went down. The Indian bullet had missed the captain, but his horse was killed. A Ranger ran up to the wounded Indian before he could reload. He seized the weapon from the Comanche's hands and used it as a club. This time, the Indian was dead.

The other Indians fled into the thick cedar, abandoning their horses and everything else.

Also left behind was a mule. Tied to it was a small boy wrapped in a buffalo robe.

Captain Tumlinson rode back to Hornsby's station on the mule, holding the little boy in his arms.

"I guess it ain't too bad a trade — one Indian and one horse for a mother's only son," Smithwick mused as they headed to camp.

When the Rangers appeared, Mrs. Hibbons rushed outside Hornsby's cabin.

"We've got your baby," the captain told her.

Many of the Rangers began studying their boots. When the captain handed the woman the only one left in her family, Jason heard several throats clearing. Jason did not see a single pair of dry eyes as mother and son were reunited.

Later that night, Captain Tumlinson approached Jason.

"Son, I was right smart busy with them Indians, but I saw how you handled your horse and that rifle. I reckon you'll do for a Ranger."

*   *   *   *   *

Captain Tumlinson and his Rangers left the young widow at Hornsby's cabin and rode northwest toward Brushy Creek. About three miles south of present-day Leander, the Rangers built a log fort that came to be called Tumlinson's blockhouse. They stayed there, guarding the frontier from Indians, until March 1836, when Texas' quest for independence from Mexico boiled over into open revolution. With the Mexican general Santa Anna marching on San Antonio and the Alamo, Tumlinson's Rangers withdrew to Bastrop. The Indians later burned the blockhouse to the ground.

At Bastrop, Maj. R. M. Williamson took over command of the Rangers. Tumlinson left to see to the protection of his own family. Like many of the early-day Rangers, Tumlinson would ride again, when needed.

Williamson fought with Sam Houston at the Battle of San Jacinto on April 21, 1836, the military victory that bought Texas' freedom. Texas was now an independent republic, but its troubles were far from over.

2

Capt. Jack Hays:
"Bravo Too Much"

By the spring of 1840, Texas had been an independent republic for four years. The Republic had little money in its treasury, but its leaders knew it was very important to provide what money they could for frontier defense. Danger lurked at each point of the compass. To the south was the constant threat of Mexican invasion. To the west and north were hostile Indians. In the east, the area of heaviest settlement, there was a serious problem with Cherokee Indians and a bloody feud between two bitter factions of settlers that nearly boiled into open warfare.

Though officially known either as "spies," "volunteer companies," "militia," "mounted gunmen," or "detachment of troops," the men who protected the young republic continued to add to the Ranger tradition. The Rangers also were changing from a mostly unpaid force to a service provided by the government.

The most famous Ranger of the 1840s was a young surveyor from Tennessee, John Coffee Hays.

*   *   *   *   *

The moon was so bright it looked like someone with a mighty long reach had hung a Texas-size lantern up there in the sky.

The Alamo, the old Spanish mission where a handful of Texans had held off Santa Anna for thirteen days back during the revolution, stood silver-plated in the moonlight. The crumbling fortress was dark and empty, but there was life elsewhere in San Antonio de Bexar.

Capt. Jack Hays and his Rangers were guests at a grand *baile,* a dance thrown in honor of the young Rangers and their vigorous recent work against the Comanches.

Hays, wearing a frock coat instead of his usual buckskin, skipped across the dance floor with a pretty, dark-haired *señorita*. His other Rangers stood outside the *cantina,* awaiting their turn to join the party. The Rangers had been able to come up with only one coat between them. They had decided to share. The captain got to go first.

The pounding of horse hooves got the waiting Rangers' minds off the party.

The rider was breathing as hard as his horse. "Is Captain Hays inside?" he managed to ask.

"Who asks?" one of the Rangers challenged, touching the butt of his long pistol, just in case.

"There's Indians afoot. I must talk with the captain if he's here."

Another of the Rangers spoke up. "I reckon he won't mind being disturbed with Indian news. Meantime, I expect we may as well start saddling up."

The rider burst into the *cantina.* "Captain Hays . . . The Comanches are just west of here, driving off most of the horses and mules in Bexar."

The music stopped. Talk and laughter died away.

"How many are there?"

"I figure two hundred if there's a one. They hit right after the moon come up."

The captain bowed to his dancing partner. "*Señorita,*

15

if you will excuse me, my men and I have some business to attend to. I shall hope to make your acquaintance again."

By the time the captain stepped outside into the cool night air, his men were on their horses. One of them held the captain's mount.

"Fast work, boys. Let's ride!"

*   *   *   *   *

The Rangers had no problem picking up the trail. The messenger had not been exaggerating: A large party of Indians had boldly raided the western fringes of town.

They rode hard for several miles before they could see and hear the Indians driving the stolen stock in the distance. As the Rangers spurred their horses, the Indians splashed across the Guadalupe River.

"Boys, yonder are the horse thieves, and there are the stolen horses. They are ten to one against us, but we can whip 'em! What do you say?"

"Fight 'em!" one of the Rangers shouted. "You lead, and we'll be right behind you!"

The captain ordered the men to dismount, tighten their saddle cinches, and check their weapons.

Hays was not concerned about the element of surprise. As the Rangers readied for their charge, the Indians realized they had been followed and began spreading out on the other side of the river.

"Come on, boys!" Hays yelled, spurring his horse to the gallop.

The Rangers splashed across the river through a wave of arrows they could hear but not see. Now practically on top of the Indians, the Rangers began firing.

Men and horses screamed. The ferocity of the charge pushed the Rangers through and beyond the Indians. Many of the Indian ponies reared back on their hind legs, tumbling their painted riders to the ground. Others fell as Ranger bullets hit their mark.

The Indians tried to regroup, but panic took over. More and more fell to Ranger bullets.

One Indian who had managed to stay on his horse rode back and forth, desperately trying to hold his war party together. Shouting his battle cry, the Indian on the decorated black horse deliberately lowered his tough buffalo hide shield to draw fire.

Hays recognized this Indian as their chief, and briefly allowed himself to admire his courage under fire. Someone else's honor could be appreciated but not allowed to prevail. The chief slipped from his horse in a hail of Ranger fire.

With the chief's death, the fight was over. The Indians who could still ride fled westward, leaving their captured horseflesh behind.

Hays and his men turned back to the river and the recaptured animals.

One of the Rangers rode up to Hays, leading the dead chief's black horse.

"Look here, Cap. I know the man this horse belongs to. He reckoned his horse had wandered off, but he hadn't wandered at all. The Indians stole him."

"Let's get these animals back to town," Hays yelled.

The captain wheeled his horse around and was about to move on when he spotted something on the ground. Quickly dismounting, he reached down to pick up the slain chief's shield.

"I reckon he won't be needing it anymore."

*   *   *   *   *

The boy captain, barely twenty-four years old, still was older than most of his men. But under Hays' command, his young Rangers quickly became seasoned Indian fighters. When they were not scouting for Indians, or traveling with Hays while he handled some surveying work, the Rangers rounded up horse thieves. The outlaws who did not die fighting usually ended up hanging on the end of a rope or standing before a hastily assembled fir-

17

ing squad. Hays' authority to dispense frontier justice came directly from the president of the Republic, Sam Houston.

In 1841, the western edge of Texas was not a safe place, but Capt. Jack Hays, who had joined the Rangers at the suggestion of General Houston, was making it safer. The captain's methods were simple: He fought hard and he fought smart. He kept cool during a fight, watched what was going on around him, and took decisive action based on what he saw.

The Comanches, a people who seldom acknowledged fear, came to dread Hays' appearance. They called him "Captain Yack," the way his first name sounded to them in that strange tongue called English. A Lipan Apache who sometimes rode with Hays and knew him as friend said he was "bravo too much."

The day Captain Hays decided to climb a huge hunk of granite northwest of San Antonio called Enchanted Rock, Hays' Indian friend was nearly proven correct.

*   *   *   *   *

Visible for miles, the pink rock towered 600 feet above the surrounding country. It was far beyond the settlements, near the headwaters of the Pedernales River. From the south side, the rock had been worn by the elements over countless centuries and could be climbed, though the lower reaches were littered with granite boulders. The summit was an expanse of bald, windswept granite, pockmarked with craters that in the spring and fall held fresh rainwater and supported delicate plants. On its north side, the rock dropped sharply, far too steep to climb. For ages, the rock had offered a commanding view for animal or man, and often provided a cool drink after a hard climb. Indians considered it a sacred place. Sometimes, when the wind blew strong and cold from the north, it was said the rock itself issued deep moans. Or were the moans from spirits inside?

Hays, Lt. Henry McCulloch, and several of their men

were on a scouting and surveying expedition. They had set up camp that night on Crabapple Creek. Sentries posted away from camp kept an eye on the horses and stood guard against surprise attack. All but two of the other men, tired after a long day in the saddle, were sleeping.

The captain was cleaning his heavy five-shot Colt revolvers as Lieutenant McCulloch looked on. Finished with one, Hays slipped the well-oiled pistol into its long, leather holster.

"I may not need you, but if I do, I will need you mighty bad," Hays said in a low voice, patting the weapon.

*   *   *   *   *

Hays watched the rock change from gray to fiery orange as the sun rose.

"I believe I'll go up there for a look-see," the captain said. "Anyone want to come along?"

The other Rangers did not seem to share his fascination with the rock. It looked like a long, hard climb to them. Another cup of coffee or two seemed like a lot better idea.

"Very well, boys. I'll go up there by myself," the captain said, taking up his rifle and strapping on his two pistols and Bowie knife.

The other Rangers were dead right. Getting to the top was a hard job, even for a young man in fine shape. But the view was worth the panting. In every direction, as far as Hays could see, was nothing but wide-open country, the prettiest land any man could want. No wonder people were flocking to Texas to claim their piece of it.

Hays could have enjoyed the view for hours, but he had work to do. With one last look, he turned to head back down the steep granite mountain.

The rock was an excellent lookout point, but a man also stood out against the barren granite. A person could see for miles — but he could be seen for miles too.

19

The young Ranger captain soon discovered he was not alone on the rock. A party of at least twenty Comanche braves was moving up the rock in his direction. They were between him and camp, leaving him only one choice of action.

Scrambling his way back up the rock, Hays started looking for a place to make a stand. He found it under an overhanging rock that bridged two ledges.

Checking his weapons, he discovered he had dropped his powder horn in his hasty flight from the Comanches. That meant he had only eleven shots — one with his rifle and five from each of his two Colts.

The young Ranger did not dwell on the arithmetic, but he knew what it added up to: More Indians were after him than he had bullets for.

The Indians had not been far behind. Soon Hays saw their grinning faces peering at him over the rim of the crater he had run down into for cover. The Indians whooped with delight when they realized the man they had trapped was the hated "Captain Yack." The warrior who took his scalp would have plenty of good medicine.

Shouting "Devil Yack" and "White Devil" in English, and worse things in Spanish, the Comanches tried to get Hays mad enough to expose himself foolishly. Hays felt his blood rising, but he knew what they were trying to do. He stayed behind his cover.

The Indians were as cautious as Hays. Whenever the Ranger raised his rifle to try for a shot, the Indians ducked.

To divide his attention, several of the Indians worked their way around to the overhanging rock. Hays fired whenever he caught a glimpse of bronze skin. He soon emptied his pistol, as dead Indians rained around him.

The shooting left his ears ringing, but all else was silent. The Indians had stopped their name calling and had moved beyond his field of view. Hays knew they were getting ready to come at him head on.

One Indian grew impatient. With foolish boldness, he popped up over the rim with drawn bow. The Ranger's rifle cracked and the Comanche fell dead.

The other Comanches felt the siege had lasted long enough. With blood-chilling war cries, they leaped up and charged Hays' rock fortress. More Indians dropped as the Ranger snapped off all five rounds from his second pistol.

Out of ammunition, Hays grimly unsheathed his razor-sharp Bowie knife. If the Comanches were to have his hair, they would pay for it dearly. Crouching with the big-bladed knife at the ready, the sweetest music he had ever heard reached his ears: the Texas yells of his fellow Rangers. They had heard his shooting and had not wanted to miss out on a good fight.

The Comanches still outnumbered the Rangers, but Hays' deadly shooting and the unexpected counterattack were too much for the Indians, who left Enchanted Rock to the spirits and that white devil, "Captain Yack."

*   *   *   *   *

The story of Hays' fight at Enchanted Rock was told around many a Texas campfire. Hays had nearly a dozen documented fights with Indians, but this fight was considered his most remarkable one.

Hays became a major and the highest-ranking officer on the Republic of Texas' western frontier. When he was not out after hostile Indians or Mexicans who still did not like the idea of Texas being separate from their country, Hays stayed busy with his surveying work.

In 1845, the Republic that Hays had fought brilliantly to make a safer place was admitted to the Union.

Gen. Zachary Taylor, who later became president of the United States, brought a large force of U.S. Army troops to Texas shortly after Texas became the twenty-eighth state. Soon war broke out between the U.S. and Mexico.

Taylor wisely realized the value of experienced

fighting men who knew South Texas and the border country. He recruited several companies of Texas Rangers into federal service. One of those companies was led by Hays, whose name soon became another word for terror in Mexico. The Rangers rode as scouts ahead of the regular army units, patrolled behind the columns to guard against guerrilla attacks, and took part in the major battles. Under Hays, who had become a colonel, the Rangers fought with such ferocity they became known in Mexico as "Los Diablos Tejanos" — the Texas Devils.

One of the things that made Hays a successful Ranger was his ability to pick good men to serve with him. One of those men was a young doctor who had come to Texas from Tennessee in the summer of 1836, John Salmon Ford.

Tall, muscular, and with ruddy complexion, Ford had deep blue eyes and a noble, Roman nose. He had ridden with Hays for a time before the Mexican War, then drifted from rangering to doctoring to law to journalism. But in 1847, when Hays called for more volunteers after the capture of Monterrey, Mexico, Ford left his position as editor of the *Texas Democrat* in Austin and enlisted. Soon he was promoted to lieutenant and transferred to Hays' staff as adjutant.

One of Ford's jobs was writing reports on men killed in action. Beneath his signature on each report, Ford wrote "Rest in Peace." As the number of men who died in the war increased, Ford took to replacing "Rest in Peace" with the shorter "R.I.P." Ford also had a habit of giving his fellow Rangers nicknames. Another Ranger, thinking it was high time Ford had a nickname himself, started calling him "Old Rip" Ford. The name stuck.

After the war was over, things must have seemed too peaceful in Texas for Hays. In 1849, he led a party of gold-seekers to California. Hays became sheriff of San Francisco, served as surveyor general of California, and founded the city of Oakland. He visited Texas occasionally, but he never moved back. He died in California in 1883 at the age of sixty-six.

Hays' former adjutant, "Rip" Ford, took up where Hays left off. Before Ford's colorful Ranger career was over, many of Texas' enemies would be resting in peace themselves.

3

"Rest in Peace" Ford

The war with Mexico had been over for more than a decade, but the country below the Nueces River and above the Rio Grande was practically a no-man's land. The Rio Grande was the border between Texas and Mexico, but many in Mexico thought the proper boundary between the two countries should be the Nueces.

The Rio Grande meant nothing to Juan Nepomuceno Cortina, a red-headed Mexican with a fiery temper that fit right in with the color of his hair. He came from a respected Mexican ranching family, but he was causing trouble on the Texas side of the river around Brownsville, the southernmost city in the state. In July 1859, he shot and killed the city marshal in Brownsville and then fled across the river to Matamoros, Mexico. In late September he came back, this time seeking revenge on a group of Texans who had formed a posse to arrest him. Several Texans were killed in the shootout that followed. Cortina went back to his family ranch, where he soon had a large following of Mexican bandits as well as many Mexican-Americans eager for a fight with Texans.

The situation continued to get worse, and the Valley was virtually unprotected. U.S. Army troops normally stationed in Brownsville, Rio Grande City, and Laredo had been moved to West Texas to handle Indian problems. Realizing this, Cortina made plans to take control of Brownsville, the first step in seizing all of South Texas.

In November, the army sent a force of infantry from San Antonio to the lower border. Texas Gov. H. R. Runnels ordered several companies of Rangers to be formed in San Antonio and sent to help the federal soldiers. Neither the U.S. troops nor the poorly led Rangers from San Antonio were having much luck in corralling Cortina.

Soon, Capt. "Rip" Ford would be sent to the Valley to straighten things out.

*   *   *   *   *

"Rip" Ford, tan and weathered after months in the saddle, walked along Austin's Congress Avenue one day in early November 1859. His well-worn buckskins had been replaced with the more staid broadcloth of a city gentleman. He was intent on enjoying what civilization the frontier capital city had to offer.

Up ahead, on a hill at the head of the wide, dusty avenue, stood the state's capitol. Ford looked at the plain limestone building with the small dome on top. Only twenty years before, Ford had heard tell that a herd of buffalo had stampeded down what was now the main street of the city. Now the buffalo, and the Indians who lived on buffalo meat, roamed far to the west in the unsettled part of Texas. But even that was changing. Ford had had a hand in it.

Winter was coming on, but the legislature was still in session. The city was at its liveliest with the lawmakers in town.

As Ford moved along the sidewalk, a man waved to make sure Ford saw him and walked briskly in his direction. Ford recognized the man as Forbes Britton, the state senator from the seaport village of Corpus Christi.

"Have you heard, Captain? That bandit Cortina has invaded Corpus Christi! The town's been sacked, burned. My family . . ."

Ford knew there was trouble stirring in South Texas. The newspapers had had several reports on the exploits of Juan Nepomuceno Cortina. But Ford doubted that Cortina was bold enough to strike as far north as Corpus Christi.

"Senator, I think it highly unlikely for Cortina to venture all the way to Corpus Christi. Surely, sir, the rumor has moved faster than that scoundrel could."

The two men talked for several minutes. Ford just about had the senator calmed down when Governor Runnels walked up.

Eyes dancing, chin trembling, and voice quivering, the senator reported the rumored invasion to the governor.

The governor listened intently, though he noticed that Ford was barely containing laughter at the senator's hysterics. As Ford looked on, he noticed Governor Runnels appeared to be taking the senator more and more seriously.

Finally, the governor turned to the seasoned Indian fighter.

"Ford, you must go. You must go at once, and swiftly," he ordered.

*　　*　　*　　*　　*

The following afternoon, Ford and seven men crossed the Colorado River on the ferry at the foot of Congress Avenue and rode south from Austin. The Ranger had not bothered to wait around for the paperwork authorizing him to raise a company of Rangers, though the formal orders followed on November 17. The orders were simple. Ford was to go to the Rio Grande with his Rangers and assume overall command of the Rangers already there.

"The service required," Governor Runnels had written, "is to protect the western frontier against Cortinas [the correct spelling is without the "s"] and his band and to arrest them if possible."

Word spread quickly that Ford was headed for South Texas. Armed volunteers joined in along the way. At Goliad, near the ruins of two old Spanish missions, citizens raised money to equip the Ranger company.

Moving deeper into South Texas, Ford found that the "invasion" of Corpus Christi was only a rumor, just as he had thought. But Ford also learned that Cortina had up to 700 men under his control.

By the time Ford reached the Valley, a combined force of regular army troops and Rangers had set out after the bandit, who had been within eight miles of Brownsville. Ford and his Rangers had been spotted by a lookout in a church steeple, who thought at first Cortina and his men were headed for the city. A small force of men who had turned out to defend the town gave three hearty cheers when they realized the determined riders galloping into Brownsville were Rangers.

The Rangers could hear shooting as they rode through town, but it was not much of a fight and they missed most of it. Cortina's mounted men escaped across the river. The bandits, left without horses, stayed on the Texas side but moved farther upstream.

That night, Ford's Rangers pitched camp along with the U.S. soldiers not far from where they had had the fight earlier that day with Cortina. Ford and his men went to sleep in a chilly, steady rain. The next morning, the Ranger captain discovered most of his men's ammunition had been soaked.

"Listen to them bugles," one Ranger said. "Old Cortina still ain't far off. Looks like we're going to get a fightin' chance at him yet."

Ford would have liked to have ridden off after the bandit at that point, but he was worried about his ammunition supply. He didn't doubt that his men would hold up well in a fight, but they couldn't make a show with wet powder.

"Men, I want to pursue that rascal, but we can't throw rocks at him. We're going back to Brownsville for dry powder."

Reluctantly, Ford ordered his Rangers from the field.

At Fort Brown, Ford met with the ranking army officer, Maj. Samuel Heintzelman and another Ranger captain, William G. Tobin. The three men agreed to work together to corral Cortina. Since they had no certain knowledge of Cortina's location, they agreed to divide their men and fan out across the Valley to find the bandit.

*   *   *   *   *

The Rangers under Ford worked their way through the thick brush. Thorns tore at men and horses as they moved upriver toward Rio Grande City.

"Boys, down here in this country, if it ain't got horns, it's got thorns," one of the Rangers mused. "I'm having trouble recalling what it was made me sign up for all this."

Despite the rough going, the Rangers soon learned they were heading in the right direction. Coming up on a fresh campsite, the Rangers knew Cortina had been there the night before.

The next day, the outlaw's trail was even more evident. Charred ranch houses, burned fences, and destroyed property littered Cortina's path. The Rangers spent a lonesome Christmas out in the brush.

The day after Christmas, Ford and his Rangers made camp at Las Cuevas, eighteen miles below Rio Grande City. Meanwhile, word had filtered back to them that Cortina had taken over Rio Grande City. Most of the residents had fled for their lives, leaving the bandit free to loot the city.

That night, Ford met with the army officers. The soldiers, Ford's Rangers, and the men under Captain Tobin would move on Rio Grande City during the night. Ford's job would be to slip around the city if he could, trapping Cortina in a circle.

After about an hour, Ford's guide spotted a group of men in the brush ahead of the Rangers.

"Quien viva?" the guide shouted. "Who goes there?"

The question was answered with a shot. The bullet missed the guide, who fired back, also missing. Rangers spurred their horses in pursuit, but the men, apparently scouts for Cortina, escaped into the thick chaparral.

"It ain't any easier for them to cut through this brush than us," one of the Rangers said. "Unless they take to the road, and they're too smart for that, they're not going to get word to Cortina tonight. We can still surprise him in the morning."

By late evening, Ford had gotten as close to Rio Grande City as he felt he could. Near the abandoned army post on the edge of town, Ringgold Barracks, the Rangers bedded down for the night, sleeping on the ground with their horses' reins in their hands.

Before going to sleep, Ford did some calculating. He had ninety Rangers under his command. Cortina had at least six men for each one of his Rangers. It would be a right lively little fight!

Heavy rumbling awoke Ford before dawn. Major Heintzelman was moving his artillery down the road toward the captured city. Quickly, the Ranger captain rode to find the major.

"Cortina's camped between the river and town," Ford told the major. "I intend to try to get my men around his flank."

Still barely daylight, the Rangers moved down the road toward Rio Grande City. The bandit's outer guard saw the Rangers and rushed to report to Cortina.

When the Rangers reached Ringgold Barracks, they were met by gunfire from an advance party of Cortina's men. Blistering fire from the Rangers drove them back.

The bandit, Ford quickly learned, had pulled his

men back into a thicket of large ebony trees on a rise overlooking the town.

The Rangers moved in two columns, hoping to catch Cortina in a deadly crossfire. As the Rangers closed to within a couple of hundred yards of the bandit and his men, two cannons began blasting away at the Texans.

The Mexicans were firing grape shot — marble-sized pieces of lead designed for use against infantry — but for some lucky reason the artillery fire was not finding its mark.

As one detachment of the Rangers concentrated on the two cannons, Ford ordered a mounted charge. Rangers rode to within forty yards of the artillery, then leaped off their horses and began pouring in rifle fire.

Cannon and small-arms fire filled the air.

"Those boys of yours fight like old veterans," one admiring U.S. Army officer told Ford.

The battle continued fiercely. The fog still was so thick it was hard for either side to tell who they were shooting.

A Mexican bugler suddenly sounded the charge, and a wave of mounted bandits swept toward Ford and his men.

Bullets seemed to be coming in toward the Rangers from every direction. It looked as if they were being surrounded.

"All right, boys," Ford yelled, "we can whip them just as easy in that shape as in any other."

The Rangers beat back the bandit charge. As Cortina's men began pulling their two cannons back, the Rangers surged forward on foot.

"Mount up, boys," Ford yelled. The Rangers ran to their horses and charged after the fleeing bandits.

Many of his men lay dead on Texas soil, but Cortina and the rest of his bandits crossed the river safely into Mexico. Ford's men had not wiped out Cortina and his followers, but the battle had taught the outlaw that any further adventures on the Texas side of the river would cost him dearly.

When Ford and his Rangers rode into Rio Grande City, no one was happier to see them than an old friend of Ford's, Judge Sam Stewart.

The haggard-looking judge pumped the Ranger captain's hand. "By God, Ford, I'm pleased to see you here," he said. "Cortina had intended to stand me up in front of a firing squad this morning. I was making my final peace when I heard you urging on your men. I thought your voice was the sweetest voice I ever heard."

*   *   *   *   *

Ford and his Rangers continued to skirmish with Cortina that winter and early spring. The Rangers did what the U.S. Army could not — when necessary they crossed into Mexico in pursuit of the bandit. Men died on both sides and property damage in the Valley was considerable.

By mid-April of 1860, Texas had a new governor: Sam Houston, the hero of the Battle of San Jacinto and the first president of the Republic of Texas. Governor Houston ordered Captain Ford and another Ranger captain to disband their companies. The nervous citizens of the Valley did not like it, but a far more serious problem than the bandit Cortina was preoccupying Houston.

Southern states, including Texas, were beginning to talk about secession from the United States, a move that surely would bring about a civil war.

"Rip" Ford, admired by his men and respected and feared by his enemies, mustered his Rangers out of service, finished the necessary paperwork, and saddled up for the long ride back to Austin.

*   *   *   *   *

When the Civil War began, the U.S. Army withdrew from Texas and most of the able-bodied Texan men left to fight for the Confederacy. The Texas frontier was left unprotected, and Indians made things miserable for the hardy families who dared stay in the distant settlements and ranches.

The state government created a Frontier Regiment (its men were called Rangers) to protect the unguarded frontier. But as the bloody war drew on, most of these men were pressed into Confederate military service. The day of the volunteer, unpaid Ranger returned. By the end of the war, only young boys and old men stood between the people of Texas and Comanches, outlaws, deserters, and other undesirables.

During the period of social and political upheaval following the Civil War, more than 1,000 men were recruited to protect the Western frontier. The men were called Texas Rangers, but they were more like a volunteer cavalry than peace officers. Civil law enforcement was handled by an organization called the State Police, which became a corrupt and widely hated force under the administration of radical Gov. E. J. Davis. In the spring of 1873, after subjecting the people of Texas to many abuses, the State Police force was abolished. As the *Texas State Gazette* put it, "The police law is abolished over the Governor's veto. Glory to God in the highest; on earth peace, good will towards men."

4

The Frontier Battalion

In the days after Reconstruction, the hard times that came after the Civil War, Texas was beginning to prosper. Cowboys pushed large herds of Longhorn cattle to railheads in Kansas, reviving Texas' war-torn economy. As cattle drives snaked up the dusty trails toward the north, new settlers flocked to Texas. Railroad tracks cut across the prairie like fast-growing vines, turning once sleepy little towns into bustling centers of commerce.

The frontier crept farther and farther to the West, putting growing pressure on the remaining Indian tribes in the state. Settlers moved to the edge of the frontier at the risk of their lives.

While the problem of hostile Indians was a familiar one, the state faced another worry: an increasing amount of violent crime among its own citizens. Local law officers struggled with a growing number of murders, assaults, robberies, cattle thefts, and bloody feuds.

In 1874, Gov. Richard Coke and the legislature saw the need for a large Texas Ranger force. Five companies of Rangers — A, B, C, D, and E — each made up of seventy-five men, were organized into a force formally called the Frontier Battalion. This battalion, which would serve Texas for the next twenty-five years, was the first permanent Texas Ranger force.

The first leader of the Frontier Battalion was Maj. John B. Jones, a South Carolinian who grew up in Texas. He was a small man, standing five feet eight inches and weighing only 135 pounds. But under Jones' leadership, the Frontier Battalion tamed Texas, ridding it of its last major threat from Indians and many of the toughest outlaws in the West.

One of those outlaws was the notorious train robber Sam Bass. Major Jones personally led the search for Bass, which ended on July 20, 1878, in the small Central Texas town of Round Rock, just north of Austin. In a shootout with four Rangers, one of Bass' gang was killed outright. Bass was badly wounded but managed to escape. He was found a short distance from town, sitting under a tree. Despite the best efforts of the town's doctor, the twenty-seven-year-old Bass died a short time later. Some said his last words were: "Life is but a bubble, trouble wherever you go."

The dying young outlaw may or may not have said that, but the Texas Rangers of the Frontier Battalion seemed to find trouble wherever they went. Then they took care of it.

Another outlaw the Rangers had to deal with was a preacher's son, John Wesley Hardin.

*   *   *   *   *

Sheriff John Carnes rushed into the telegraph office, clutching his shotgun so hard his knuckles were white. He had the hammers pulled back on both barrels as he said, "Wire this to the governor immediately: Deputy killed. Lynch mob forming. Rush all Rangers possible to Comanche."

Outside, all around the limestone courthouse, milled an agitated crowd of armed men. Sheriff Carnes knew he was outnumbered and outgunned, but the buckshot in his double-barreled shotgun would at least buy a little time. The cost would be the lives of a few normally law-abiding citizens, people who had voted for him. At the moment, their passions were ablaze at the senseless killing of a deputy sheriff from neighboring Brown County. They meant Sheriff Carnes no harm — they just wanted to hang the killer. But Sheriff Carnes had to see that the man got a fair trial. That was the law and he intended to enforce it.

Folks had been streaming into Comanche all day, well before the trouble started. Comanche was a fairly young town on the far western frontier of Texas, just a collection of stores, livery stables, and saloons lining the square around the courthouse. Normally, it was a quiet town. But a big quarter horse race had brought people in from two counties for a day of spirited competition and wagering.

One of the contestants, and a big winner at the races, was the son of a Methodist preacher. On that day, May 26, 1874, John Wesley Hardin had turned twenty-one years old. Before the day was over, he would have a bullet hole in his side and a lynch mob would be howling for his neck.

For Hardin, it had started off as a mighty fine birthday. His horses won hefty purses. By the time the races were over, Hardin had collected $3,000, as well as fifty head of cattle, two wagons, and fifteen saddle horses. A man could settle down and run his own ranch with that kind of stake. But if Hardin had any notion of owning a piece of land and putting down roots, the chance died on that spring day.

Hardin and two pals, Jim Taylor and Bud Dixon, were busily celebrating in Jack Wright's saloon. Glasses clinked and coins rattled on the bar as the whiskey flowed. Hardin and his friends were drunk. He might have been a preacher's son, but as a young man Hardin had had trouble with several of the Ten Commandments, particularly "Thou shall not kill." Before his career as a gunman would come to an end, twenty-seven men would fall before his gun. Some believe the count to be even higher.

Hardin's reputation began developing in Gonzales County, southeast of Austin, during the Taylor-Sutton feud. Handy with a pistol since his teenage years, Hardin had gotten caught up in the feud, a running, bloody disagreement between two tough families and their friends.

He had come to Comanche to help out his brother Joe, a respected local attorney who also ran some cattle. In Comanche and Brown counties, it was well known that John Wesley Hardin was no ordinary cowboy.

As Hardin celebrated his birthday and his winning bets, a man packing a big Colt revolver walked toward Wright's saloon. Someone recognized him as a deputy sheriff from nearby Brown County. The deputy had no official power in Comanche County, but the six-shooter on his hip was authority enough on the Texas frontier.

Young Hardin was not a wanted man in either county, but he watched carefully as the lawman approached.

Accounts of what happened next vary. The only indisputable fact is the outcome. Some, including Hardin, said deputy Charles Webb deliberately picked a fight. Others said Hardin was mean drunk and prodded Webb into a confrontation.

Witnesses did agree on Webb's last words: "No, ——— damn you, I'm not afraid of you!"

At that, Webb drew his pistol. Unfortunately for him, the revolver went off accidentally as it cleared leather. Hardin and his friends fired so close together it sounded like one loud explosion. As the gunsmoke floated in the May breeze, Webb crumpled to the ground, hit three times.

Hardin and Taylor immediately fled, a posse close behind. Dixon decided to stay in Comanche.

When the nearest Rangers reached Comanche, they

suggested that Dixon, his brother, and Hardin's brother be placed in protective custody. Emotions of the towns-people were running high.

By June 5, Hardin and Taylor had managed to reach Austin. The same day, back in Comanche, an angry mob built up around the courthouse. Shortly after midnight, the mob stormed the jail. Joe Hardin and the Dixon brothers were led outside, ropes around their necks, and hanged from one of the live oak trees outside.

A couple of days later a friend galloped up on a tired horse to the place where Hardin and Taylor were staying west of Austin.

"Wes, the mob's killed your brother," he said. "They hanged the Dixon boys too."

The news hit the gunman like a .45 slug. He knew it would be dangerous, but he made up his mind to ride back to Comanche. A few days later, in the dead of night, he secretly visited his brother's grave. But he knew if he stayed in the county long, the next funeral would be his.

* * * * *

That October, the Comanche County Grand Jury indicted John Wesley Hardin for the murder of deputy Charles Webb. A warrant was issued for Hardin's arrest. Since the Texas Rangers had statewide authority, the job of finding Hardin rested with them.

The Rangers rounded up several of Hardin's friends and associates, but Hardin was nowhere to be found in Texas. Now an outlaw on the run, Hardin knew that the way things stood, if the Rangers did not find him, a lynch mob would.

Hardin sent his wife and infant daughter on the train to New Orleans, Louisiana, in the care of a relative. As soon as he could, he left to join up with them, traveling by horse through East Texas to New Orleans. From there, the Hardin family took a steamboat to Florida. Hardin wondered if even Florida was far enough away from the Texas Rangers. He toyed with the idea of sailing to England, but finally decided to put down roots in Florida.

Using the phony name of John H. Swain, Hardin moved his family from place to place in Florida, trying different jobs. His address changed several times, but he made sure his subscription to the *Galveston News* was current. He wanted to keep up with what was going on back in Texas, especially the Rangers' search for its most wanted outlaw, John Wesley Hardin. Rewards offered for his arrest totaled $4,000. A man could live high on the hog for years with that much money.

The fugitive in Florida was amused to read that he was still being seen in Texas. Various crimes were blamed on "Hardin and his gang." In the fall of 1875, police in Dallas mistakenly shot and killed a man they had been led to believe was Hardin. The real Hardin, of course, was hundreds of miles away.

Still, nervous Texans were reporting they had seen Hardin. Someone told Ranger John B. Armstrong that the outlaw could be found in a certain saloon, brazenly having a drink. Armstrong and a local officer hurried to the place to make the arrest. The Ranger sauntered up to the man at the bar and offered to buy him a drink. When the other officer grabbed the man's arm, Armstrong poked his cocked pistol into the man's stomach and informed him he was under arrest. Unfortunately, the prisoner was not John Wesley Hardin.

Armstrong, who took a fair amount of kidding from his fellow Rangers over his arrest of the wrong man, asked his captain for permission to devote his efforts full-time to tracking the gunman down. Capt. Lee Hall gave the go-ahead, but both men knew it would not be easy. John Wesley Hardin seemed to have vanished as quickly as a West Texas mirage.

One day in March 1877, when the train pulled into Dallas from Austin, Ranger Captain Hall stepped from one of the cars. Dallas was a wild and woolly railroad center, practically as rough as the nearby cowtown of

Fort Worth. The captain had told friends he was going north to visit relatives in Sherman, but he had something else in mind as he walked away from the railroad station.

Hall had heard about a young Dallas police officer, Jack Duncan, who had a reputation as a manhunter. The captain wanted to see if Duncan looked like Ranger material. Hall was impressed. On July 15, 1877, the twenty-six-year-old Duncan enlisted as a Ranger private under the captain. He was assigned to work with Armstrong to find Hardin.

*   *   *   *   *

Not long after Duncan went to work for the Rangers, a stranger showed up in Gonzales looking for work. The man told anyone who was interested enough to ask that his name was Williams. He hinted darkly he had had some trouble elsewhere in the state, but would just as soon not talk about it. Williams nevertheless was a likeable sort, and soon had developed a casual friendship with a man who ran a small grocery, Neal Bowen. Bowen did not bring it up in conversation with Williams, but he was Hardin's father-in-law.

Williams mostly seemed interested in getting work. Before long, he was doing day labor on farms in the area and got the word around that he was looking for a place to stay. Bowen offered to take him in as a boarder.

Williams was interested in going into business for himself, and talked with Bowen about renting a storehouse he owned. The young man had noticed a wagon on Bowen's property and asked if it was for sale. Bowen curtly said he could not sell the wagon because it belonged to someone else. He did not offer to say who that was.

Williams seemed barely interested.

"Well," he said, "it ain't much of a wagon, I guess. But if you think about it, why don't you write the fellow that owns it and see if he wants to part with it? That wagon's not doing anybody any good just sitting there."

Bowen did not realize it, but Williams was paying a lot of attention to just about everything he did. In fact, "Williams" was actually Texas Ranger Jack Duncan.

A few days after their talk about the wagon, the undercover Ranger noticed that Bowen got a letter, which he read and then quickly placed in his trunk. As soon as he could, Duncan slipped into Bowen's room and dug the letter from the trunk. It was from his son, Hardin's brother-in-law. Though the letter was worded carefully, the son said, "My sister joins me in sending love to all."

Duncan's eyes widened as he read that line. The sister, Jane Bowen, was John Wesley Hardin's wife. According to the letter, she had had a baby, the couple's third, the very day Duncan had been sworn in as a Ranger. He was right on track. John Wesley Hardin's father-in-law knew where the Hardins were hiding! Now Duncan had to figure out how to find out too.

A few days later, Bowen and "Williams" rode to nearby Cuero in DeWitt County to pick up some supplies. On the way, Duncan pulled out a whiskey bottle and offered Bowen a drink. Before long, the two were laughing and singing as they headed toward Cuero.

Duncan got serious for a moment. "When are you going to get me a price on that wagon in your yard?"

Bowen, brimming with human kindness and the false warmth of whiskey, said he would post the letter from Cuero.

"Oh, all you have to do is write it," Duncan offered. "I'll even give you an envelope and buy you a drink while you write it."

Unknown to Bowen, Duncan had previously marked the envelope for future reference.

Bowen wrote the letter, sealed it in the envelope, and dropped it in the slot at the small Cuero post office. He then went to buy the needed supplies. Duncan said he needed to tend to some other business and stayed behind.

The Ranger doubled back to the post office as soon as Bowen was gone.

All smiles, Duncan told the postmaster he had just mailed a letter but was afraid he had written the wrong address on it. The postmaster let him look into the letter bin and he quickly spotted the marked letter.

"I need to add a few lines too," Duncan smiled as he opened the letter. The Ranger quickly read the letter, re-sealed it, and dropped it back in the box. It was addressed to "Mr. J. H. Swain, Pollard, Alabama, in care of Neil McMillan."

A short time later, Duncan sent a message to Ranger Armstrong, using a code they had worked out before he went to Gonzales: "Come get your horse."

On August 15, Armstrong and several other Rangers galloped into town. "Williams" was arrested with great show, chained, and loaded into a wagon. At Cuero, the Rangers marched their "prisoner" onto the train for Austin.

Neal Bowen did not know what kind of trouble "Williams" was in, but he was sorry to see him go. He kind of liked the young man.

* * * * *

Back in Austin, Armstrong asked Adjutant General William Steele to get him two arrest warrants for Hardin: one in the outlaw's real name and one for "Swain," just in case. But Rangers Armstrong and Duncan did not wait for the warrants. On August 18, they left Austin by train, headed east. Two days later, they were in Montgomery, Alabama.

Duncan, posing as a tramp in threadbare clothes, went to the community of Pollard, located just across the state line from Florida. He soon learned J. H. Swain had gone to Pensacola, Florida, to gamble with several friends. The undercover Ranger then wired Armstrong to get to Pollard as fast as he could. From there, the two Rangers went by train to Pensacola.

41

Once in Pensacola, the Rangers checked around and found that Swain had bought a ticket for the evening train back to Pollard. The Rangers then went to the local sheriff's office.

"Sheriff," Armstrong explained, "we're here to take a gentleman who goes by the name J. H. Swain back to Texas. In Texas, we know him as John Wesley Hardin. The governor is preparing warrants for his arrest on a charge of murder. We're going to need your help. I don't expect Mr. Hardin figures to return to Texas voluntarily."

The sheriff had seen the wanted circulars. Hardin's reputation as a ruthless killer was well known to him, but he had not suspected J. H. Swain. In fact, one of his deputies had been playing cards with the man! Together, the Rangers and the sheriff worked out a plan.

*   *   *   *   *

When Hardin and several of his friends arrived at the train station, they were not alarmed to see the sheriff and several of his deputies. Lawmen routinely checked trains as they came through their towns. The two Rangers stayed out of sight.

The outlaw was in a fine mood. Just like that day in Comanche three years earlier, he had won big. Only this time, his winnings came at the gaming table, not the horse track.

Hardin and his buddies took seats in the smoking car. Hardin's back was to the door. The men had been carrying shotguns, which was perfectly legal, but had placed them in the luggage racks over their seats.

Puffing on his pipe, Hardin rested his arms on the back of his seat and settled in for the train ride back to Alabama. The sheriff and one of his deputies walked through the car, looking over the passengers. Unknown to Hardin, Ranger Armstrong was in the adjoining baggage car, with his gun drawn.

Suddenly, the sheriff and his deputy came back into

42

the smoking car through the door they had just walked through.

"I believe I want you," the sheriff said, grabbing Hardin.

Hardin, no longer all smiles, cursed and then kicked the officer. The outlaw tried to stand up but fell backwards as the sheriff slapped him in the face with his pistol.

The outlaw then began proclaiming his innocence, telling the sheriff he had made a mistake, that he had broken no law.

But then Rangers Armstrong and Duncan burst into the car, their revolvers drawn.

"Texas, by God!" Hardin said, recognizing Armstrong's big Colt as the weapon favored by Texas Rangers.

As Hardin continued to struggle with the Florida sheriff, Armstrong demanded that he surrender.

Hardin cursed, telling Armstrong to go ahead and shoot him. "I'd rather die than be arrested."

But Armstrong wanted Hardin back in Texas for a trial, not a funeral. That could come after a jury made its decision. Instead of shooting, the Ranger crashed his heavy pistol down on Hardin's head. Hardin crumpled to the railroad car floor, out cold.

One of Hardin's friends, possibly not even realizing who he had been keeping company with, pulled a pistol and fired at the Ranger. The shot missed Armstrong, but the man went down in a volley of fire.

*   *   *   *   *

The outlaw career of John Wesley Hardin was over, thanks to the Texas Rangers. The two Rangers quickly brought their notorious prisoner back to Texas. He was convicted and spent the next eighteen years behind bars. But Hardin was not destined to die of old age. He had studied law in prison, and after his release, he worked as an attorney in Gonzales before moving out to El Paso in far West Texas. Though he knew the letter of the law, his court of last resort was still the six-gun. In 1895, he was gunned down in an El Paso saloon.

5

McNelly's Rangers

The same year the legislature created the Frontier Battalion of Rangers, it created another force of Rangers to deal with problems along Texas' border with Mexico. This organization, under Capt. Leander H. McNelly, was called the Special Force of Rangers.

McNelly recruited his Rangers in Washington County, in East Texas. After he had his men together, McNelly headed to DeWitt County, in South Texas, to deal with the so-called Sutton-Taylor feud. The feud was really open warfare between two rival groups. Arriving on August 1, 1874, McNelly's Rangers began helping local law-enforcement officers, who had been unable to stop the bloodshed in the county. Rangers provided protection for judges, prosecutors and witnesses, made numerous arrests, and eventually brought law and order back to the violence-torn county.

From DeWitt County, McNelly and his Rangers rode toward the border, where bandits continued to make it unsafe for Texas citizens.

Young George Durham had ridden his plow horse from Georgia clear to Texas. All he had was a beat-up old saddle, the sweat-stained clothes he wore, a hat that was falling to pieces, and a long-barreled pistol. Washington County, Texas, was cotton country, like much of the rest of the South. He could have gotten a farm job in Georgia, but the strapping farm boy wanted something more. Trouble was, he did not exactly know what it was he wanted.

The Civil War had left Georgia in terrible shape. Much of Durham's home state had literally been burned to the ground by Gen. William T. Sherman and his Yankee troops. Texas, though it had also sided with the South, had escaped the worst of the fighting. To Durham, it seemed like the right kind of place to make a start — at something.

About the only thing Durham had in mind was looking up a man his father had told him about — Capt. Leander H. McNelly. The South had lost the war, but not because of the bantam weight McNelly. He had fought with distinction in Louisiana and Mississippi, often behind the enemy lines. One of the men he had led in battle was Durham's father.

After the war, McNelly, only twenty-one years old, returned to Texas as a hero. He had survived four years of bitter fighting, but lost his health to galloping consumption — tuberculosis, a lung disease. A religious man, McNelly settled down to the life of a gentleman cotton farmer in Washington County.

The war had been over for ten years, but most folks still called McNelly "Captain." Durham rode to the post office-general store and learned that McNelly would be by before long. The talkative postmaster said the captain had gotten an important-looking letter from the governor's office in Austin. He said the captain would probably be stopping by the store on his way to Austin.

The Georgia farm boy was sipping a soda when a

small man with a goatee walked inside, nodded politely to all, and asked for some cigars. Durham slipped up to the postmaster. "Was that little man buying the cigars really the famous Confederate cavalryman?" he asked. Durham thought the postmaster was pulling his leg at first.

The young man learned quickly that McNelly was not much on casual conversation. Outside the post office, Durham hailed the captain as he got up on his buggy, an unlit cigar clinched in his teeth.

"Captain McNelly . . . I'm George Durham, from Georgia."

McNelly stared down, his blue eyes glaring. "What can I do for you?"

"My dad worked for you in Louisiana."

"Did he get back?"

"Yes, sir, but Sherman got him."

The captain's only reply was "Uh-huh."

At that, he motioned to his driver to get along and the buggy rolled off behind two sturdy mules. Durham watched as McNelly's buggy headed off in a cloud of dust for the state capital.

For a moment, Durham considered going back to Georgia. But he had left for Texas to make a new start, and he decided to stick with it. Not having any other good ideas at the time, Durham found a job on a cotton farm there in Washington County.

With his first week's pay in his pocket, he was back at the small general store enjoying another cold soda and talking with the postmaster when he learned some interesting news: Captain McNelly had returned from Austin and had set up a camp a few miles out of town. He was hiring men to ride with him as Texas Rangers.

Durham knocked down the rest of his soda, collected his change, and headed for his horse.

About three miles out, Durham spotted a white tent pitched under a big oak tree. A group of men stood around a table outside the tent. The captain, with another one of those unlit cigars in his mouth, paced around the camp.

Durham rode his horse up to the captain and stared at him. The captain returned the gaze for a moment.

"You're the lad from Georgia?"

"Yes, sir."

"You want to sign on?"

"Yes, sir."

"Do you own a horse and saddle?"

"Yes, sir."

"Do you own that pistol you're wearing?"

"Yes, sir."

"Can you hit a target at thirty paces?"

"Meaning a man, sir?"

"Certainly."

"I don't know, sir. I never tried."

The captain sized up the farm boy for a moment. Then he nodded.

The pay would be $33 a month and food. The State of Texas would also furnish the ammunition.

After the papers were filled out, Durham milled around his fellow Rangers trying to make conversation. He did not come up with much talk, but he learned a little about what all the fuss was over — Mexican bandits were forgetting that the international boundary with Texas was the Rio Grande. They were making raids deep into Texas and stealing cattle just like it was part of Mexico.

*   *   *   *   *

McNelly moved his Rangers down into Nueces County on Corpus Christi Bay. The Ranger captain learned that bandits had raided the area less than a month before. A Mexican who had refused to join the raiders had been hanged by the rest of the bandits. Another man's wife had been beaten with a quirt by an American outlaw riding with the bandits. Eighteen expensive saddles, decorated with silver *conchos,* had been stolen by the bandits.

The merchant who lost the saddles told the Rangers he was expecting a new shipment soon and would show them what the saddles looked like when they arrived. McNelly settled for a verbal description. He politely asked the merchant not to sell any of the new saddles for a while. Then he turned to his sergeant.

"Describe those saddles to the Rangers," the captain ordered. "Make sure they understand exactly. Then empty them saddles on sight. No palavering with the riders. Leave the men where you drop them and bring the saddles to camp."

Durham, seeing the captain in action, was already beginning to understand why McNelly had been such trouble to the Yankees during the war. He also realized why the governor of Texas thought the captain was the man to handle the bandit problem.

Merchants and ranchers in South Texas also realized McNelly was the right man for the job. They outfitted his Rangers with single-shot Sharps .50-caliber rifles, the arm favored by buffalo hunters. Bandits often carried more modern repeating rifles, but the Sharps were reliable, accurate, and deadly at long range. When Durham and the other McNelly Rangers rode out of Corpus Christi that spring of 1875, they had a wagon load of ammunition.

Now that the Rangers had plenty of rifles and shells, their next problem was horseflesh. Durham and many of the other men were riding farm animals, not the strong, high-spirited kind of horse needed to chase bandits. Rancher Richard C. King, whose sprawling ranch was losing a lot of stock to the bandits, gladly furnished McNelly and his men fine horses. The captain was given the best, a tall, wide-chested bay named "Segal."

McNelly, ever the gentleman, protested the expensive gift. The State of Texas could never reimburse King for such a horse, he said.

"I'd rather give him to you than have those bandits come and take him," the rancher told the Ranger captain.

*   *   *   *   *

Well-mounted and well-armed, McNelly and his men moved deep into South Texas. At a camp not far from the Rio Grande, McNelly awaited word from a group of his Rangers that had been sent out after a party of bandits. The raiders were said to be headed south toward the river, pushing a herd of stolen stock.

The Rangers came back into camp on winded horses.

"We missed," McNelly's lieutenant started. "They were across the . . ."

The captain stood abruptly. "That's fine," he said curtly. He did not want to hear any more. He wanted results, not excuses.

Those results would not be long in coming.

*   *   *   *   *

McNelly knew from his military experience that no armed force, cavalry or Rangers, was effective without accurate intelligence — information on the strength and movements of the enemy. The information McNelly needed came from a solitary bandit captured by a couple of the Rangers.

The Rangers had spotted him astride one of the fancy saddles stolen outside of Corpus Christi. Rather than shoot him on sight, as the captain had ordered if the Rangers saw anyone on one of the stolen saddles, the Rangers decided McNelly might want to ask him a few questions on the whereabouts of the other bandits.

At first, the man claimed he had won the saddle in a poker game and knew nothing about bandits. McNelly had been sworn in to clean up South Texas. He intended to do that, even if he had to play rough. The captured bandit eventually started talking.

Some fifty bandits, leading more than 300 head of stolen stock, were moving along the coastline, headed for Mexico. McNelly intended to interfere with their plans.

That night, the Rangers settled down to dry camp —
no coffee or food. They would be leaving early in the
morning.

*   *   *   *   *

Before dawn, McNelly, Durham, and the other Rangers were riding through the low coastal scrub brush,
their horses occasionally splashing through a salt marsh.

The sun was beginning to burn off a low fog that
hung over the ground when Durham saw the scout ride
in with news that he had found the bandit's fresh trail.

The Rangers, riding two abreast behind the captain,
followed the scout at a lope down the trail. After making
a couple of miles, Durham saw the guide ride up on some
high ground, rein in his horse, and circle his hand. The
young Ranger knew what that meant as well as the experienced captain did: They were on the bandits.

As Durham watched, McNelly kicked his horse and
galloped up to the scout. The captain pulled his spyglass
from his saddlebag and looked over the situation.

The bandits had spotted the Rangers. Waving their
hats and yelling, the outlaws tried to push their stolen
stock faster. The Rio Grande was not far ahead.

McNelly put his spyglass back and hefted his pistol
from its holster. Durham could see him open the cylinder,
check to see that all chambers were loaded, and expertly
flick it closed. Seeing the other Rangers doing the same,
Durham reached for his own pistol. He was "fixing to
need it," he reckoned.

The Ranger captain turned in his saddle to make
sure his men were ready, then dug his spurs into the side
of his big King Ranch horse. Segal shot toward the bandits, the Rangers following as fast as they could ride.

The bandits had moved onto an island in the middle
of a *resaca,* still about 500 yards from the Rangers. Mc-
Nelly reined in his hard-breathing horse and walked
Segal back around to face the other Rangers.

Durham listened to his orders, his heart flopping

50

like a catfish out of water. The orders were to the point: Ride five paces apart. Don't shoot until the captain does. Don't shoot to either side, only straight ahead.

The bandits surely were not holding their fire, no matter the distance. Their bullets were splashing harmlessly into the water of the *resaca*.

Suddenly, it sank in on Durham: Those cow thieves were hoping to kill him!

McNelly seemed to pay no attention to the shooting. He headed Segal into the water and the Rangers followed.

The boldness of the Rangers caught the bandits by surprise. The bandits had had time to position themselves behind cover. They did not expect the Rangers to keep coming straight at them.

McNelly and his Rangers continued to ride toward the bandits, who started shooting more. Still the Rangers kept coming, riding as if they were bullet-proof. The Rangers continued to hold their fire as the captain had ordered.

The Ranger determination was too much for some of the bandits. They ran from cover and jumped on their horses. Others held their ground and kept shooting at the Rangers.

A horse screamed. One of the Rangers jumped from the saddle as his wounded horse fell. A few other horses were raring back, also hit by the outlaw fire. Then Durham's horse was hit, dropping to its knees in the mud. Durham held tightly to his carbine and leaped into the water of the *resaca*. Fear gripped the young Georgian even tighter. Bullets whined past him.

McNelly continued to hold his fire. Now only thirty paces from the bandits, the Ranger captain aimed his revolver and squeezed the trigger. An outlaw pitched forward. The other Rangers cut loose with their carbines or pistols.

Durham saw a hat behind a clump of salt cedar. The outlaw was rising to run. Durham aimed his carbine and fired. When the smoke cleared, the outlaw was on the ground.

The bandits who had stood their ground were thinking better of it now. They scrambled for their mounts, but it was too late. McNelly's men had stayed in line, shooting only at those in front of them. The effect was devastating.

The shooting was dying down now. McNelly moved slowly toward a patch of marsh grass about ten paces away. The captain had seen an outlaw firing from the spot moments before. The outlaw had quit shooting, but McNelly did not think he was dead.

"My pistol's empty," McNelly shouted back toward the other Rangers. "Bring me some more shells."

The outlaw fell for the trick. He rose from the grass, a wide-bladed knife in his hand and a snarl on his face.

McNelly's pistol was not empty. The outlaw looked puzzled as he sank to the ground, fatally wounded.

The captain got back on his horse and surveyed the scene. Most of the shooting had died down. In the distance, he saw his lieutenant motioning for him to come over.

McNelly's second-in-command was standing over a wounded bandit.

"He's asking for a chaplain," the lieutenant said.

The captain got off his horse, put his revolver back in its holster, and pulled a small Bible from his jacket. He leaned down over the dying man and read quietly to him until he died.

The bodies of dead outlaws were scattered all over the *resaca*. The Rangers had not lost a man.

Suddenly, an outlaw who must have been trying to hide jumped from the grass toward a horse. Two Rangers fired and he went down. One of the Rangers walked over to take a look. The dying outlaw managed to fire one shot, killing the young Ranger.

Back in Brownsville, McNelly ordered the bodies of the bandits displayed in the town square as a warning to others. The slain Ranger was buried with full military honors.

*   *   *   *   *

George Durham rode with the captain and his men until a new governor disbanded McNelly's special force. The fight on the *resaca* had marked the turning point in the state's efforts to make South Texas as safe as the rest of the state. Not for another forty years would the Rangers be needed in the Rio Grande Valley as badly as they were when McNelly rode through the brush in the mid-1870s.

Durham, the Georgia farm boy, became a man in South Texas and he stayed there. He went to work for the King Ranch, married one of Capt. Richard King's nieces, and lived there the rest of his days. He lived to be an old man, but always looked back at his Rangering days under McNelly as the finest years of his life.

6

The Lone Star Ranger: Capt. John R. Hughes

The men of Capt. George W. Baylor's Ranger company had been up before dawn and now moved stealthily up the crest of one of the Diablo mountains in far West Texas. In the mountain cold, the breath of the Rangers turned to steam. The Rangers had been on the trail of a band of Apaches that had killed a stagecoach driver and a passenger earlier in the month. The Pueblo Indian scouts working for the Rangers had spotted the Apache camp, and Baylor was positioning his men to attack. The Rangers got within a hundred yards of the Indians before they were spotted. By that time, it was too late for the Apaches.

The Rangers broke the early-morning silence with their Springfield and Winchester rifles. In a few moments, it was over. Six Indians were killed. The few surviving Indians escaped on foot, though the Rangers took one squaw and two Apache children as prisoners. The Rangers captured about forty head of horses, which they believed had been stolen, along with several rifles, pistols, and U.S. Cavalry saddles. Captain Baylor ordered that everything else the Indians left behind be burned. The Rangers then settled down to eat the breakfast the Indians had been cooking.

The fight took place on January 29, 1881. For the Rangers, it was a routine day's work, but the brief battle turned out to be the last Indian fight in Texas. The frontier was fading. The Indian and the buffalo, their primary food supply, were gone from Texas. In 1882, the Southern Pacific Railroad was completed across West Texas, and with the Indian threat gone, settlers poured in from the east.

For the first time in their history the Rangers did not have to worry about hostile Indians. But the men of the Frontier Battalion still had plenty of work to do. Cattle thieves preyed on the big ranches that were springing up in the grass-rich highlands of the Trans-Pecos. Criminals of all classes were following the railroad into West Texas. The good grazing lands were being fenced off by private landowners with barbed wire, a recent invention that created a new type of law-enforcement problem: fence-cutting. Many cattlemen felt the range should be open to all, no matter what might be written on a piece of paper filed at the courthouse. They cut the barbed wire and went their way, just as they had always been able to do in Texas. But fence-cutting was against the law.

Ranger Ira Aten, frustrated in his efforts to stop fence-cutting, came up with a novel idea typical of the Ranger way of thinking. He put out the word, which spread across Texas like a prairie fire: If folks did not start respecting the newfangled barbed wire fences, Aten would booby trap them with dynamite so they would explode when someone snipped the wire. Aten's superiors quickly overruled the dynamite scheme, but the problem soon died down thanks to the efforts of Aten and other Rangers.

Another Frontier Battalion Ranger of note was John R. Hughes, who had joined the force in 1887. By the early

1890s, Hughes was in Company D, which was then assigned to far West Texas.

* * * * *

Ranger Cpl. John R. Hughes reined in his horse and stood in the saddle for a moment to stretch his legs. He knew that the mountains towering in the distance, and the desert trail he was following, were in New Mexico. As he watched, the mountains were turning from purple to black in the late afternoon shadows. The harder he rode toward the jagged peaks, he thought, the farther away they seemed to be.

Somewhere in this part of New Mexico Territory was an outlaw named Geronimo Parra. Ranger Hughes had been on his trail for days. Parra had gunned down one of Hughes' fellow Rangers back near El Paso, and Hughes intended to see that Parra got back to Texas to face the hangman's rope.

Hughes knew he had no real authority outside of Texas, but if he found Parra, the outlaw would be going back to El Paso with him, one way or the other. The Ranger did not much care whether Parra returned to Texas sitting in a saddle or came back dead, draped sideways over his horse.

The Ranger had had a good trail to follow, but eventually the outlaws had split up. Hughes had no way of knowing which set of hoof prints belonged to Parra's horse. So, giving up a direct pursuit, Hughes had been moving from ranch to ranch, anywhere a few people could be found, and passing the word that he wanted Geronimo Parra. Several people had told him Parra had been seen in and around Las Cruces, an old New Mexico settlement about forty miles north of El Paso.

At Las Cruces, a collection of sun-baked adobe buildings in the badlands of Southwestern New Mexico, the Ranger checked with local officers. No one seemed to know where Parra could be found.

Frustrated, the Ranger went to the telegraph office

and wired his boss, Capt. Frank Jones. The captain and most of the other Rangers of Company D, Frontier Battalion, were in camp at Alpine, 200 miles east of El Paso. After sending the message, the tired Ranger took his horse to the livery stable and went to look for something to eat until he heard back from his captain.

Captain Jones' return wire ordered Hughes to get back to the Ranger camp in Alpine as soon as possible. Another assignment awaited him, though the captain did not say in the brief telegraph what the Ranger's next job would be.

Hughes looked again at the brief message scrawled on the telegraph form and then wadded it up and tossed it down. He did not like the idea of leaving the killer of a fellow Texas Ranger at large, but orders were orders. As soon as his horse was rested up enough to ride, he would head back to El Paso. But he would not forget about Geronimo Parra.

*   *   *   *   *

El Paso was a lively little town on the Rio Grande at the far western tip of Texas, a favorite stopping place for weary western travelers. Hughes liked the city in the mountain pass and had many friends there, but with his orders to report to Alpine, the Ranger did not linger. As soon as he could get on an east-bound train, he was headed for the Ranger camp. His horse made the trip in a livestock car.

On the train, Corporal Hughes had time to catch up on his reading. The *El Paso Times,* which, like other frontier papers, got much of its news from other newspapers, had several stories on the goings on at Shafter, a boom town in the Big Bend.

A silver mine there was producing quality ore. Where a short time before there had been nothing, a town of 1,200 or more had sprung up like a wildflower after a rare desert rainstorm. Shafter teemed with mine workers and businessmen and the lower elements of humanity, who always seemed to show up where there was easy money to be made. Saloons and gambling houses did a brisk business. The town was growing fast, and so was its graveyard. Barroom shootings were as common as dust devils.

When Corporal Hughes reported to Captain Jones, he was not surprised to learn his new assignment had something to do with Shafter.

"John, someone's stealing ore from that mine about as fast as they can dig it out," the captain said. "It's been going on now for several months and the loss is adding up in a hurry. The mine owners have hired some detectives, but the stealing has not stopped. I've sent two of our men down there, and they haven't been able to get to the bottom of it, either."

The captain sized up the tall, heavy-set Ranger. Corporal Hughes wore a Mexican *sombrero,* a white shirt, and duck pants held up by suspenders. His pant legs were stuffed into the tops of his shiny boots. In addition to the six-shooter on his hip, the Ranger cradled a Winchester Model 94 in his arms. He seldom went anywhere without the lever-action rifle in his hands, which he carried as casually as a man back East might tote an umbrella.

"The governor told me to put the best man I could on this case — and I have," the captain said.

The train ride from El Paso to Alpine only took a few hours, but the Big Bend stretched for another hundred miles below Alpine. Shafter, sixty miles away in Presidio County, could only be reached by stagecoach or horseback. The trip to the wide-open mining town took the Ranger two days.

Once in Shafter, Corporal Hughes went straight to the mine and called on the superintendent. Hughes got right down to business.

"If we are going to catch the men who are stealing your ore, I've got to have your help," the Ranger said.

"Corporal, I've paid private detectives to find the thieves and I've already talked to two other Rangers who haven't had any luck in our behalf," the superintendent said. "So far those detectives haven't managed to find anything but the cook shack. I've had quite enough of professional coffee-coolers."

The Ranger thanked the superintendent for his time and left the mine office.

For two weeks, Hughes kept pretty much to himself, studying the mining operation and scouting the trails leading south from the mine toward Mexico — the direction the Ranger suspected the stolen silver ore was heading.

Despite the mine superintendent's attitude, the Ranger did manage to inspect the mine's payroll records. He was checking to see if any known criminals were working at the mine. His eyes stopped on a name under the S's on the list: "Diamond Dick" St. Leon. St. Leon was an ex-Texas Ranger. He had not left the force because he was a bad Ranger — St. Leon got drunk all the time. Not all Rangers on the frontier were tee-totallers, but when St. Leon started drinking, he could not stop. His friends had tried to help him, but St. Leon had been fired from the Rangers.

Hughes hoped St. Leon had not fallen in with the thieves and he did not think so. The Ranger believed St. Leon was basically a good man. He decided to give the ex-Ranger a chance to clear his name.

Until he could identify the thieves, Hughes hoped to at least cut down on the ore theft by keeping himself highly visible around the mine. Periodically, the Ranger strolled casually around the mine property, his ever-present Winchester cradled in his arm.

On one of those walks, the Ranger spotted St. Leon. The former Ranger immediately recognized Hughes.

Careful that no one else could hear him, Hughes whispered: "Meet me in the old cemetery at nine tonight." St. Leon nodded.

*   *   *   *   *

The graveyard was on the edge of town, up on a rise. Hughes went there early and sat quietly in the dark, .30-.30 in hand. Laughter and music drifted over from the distant saloons, but the graveyard was as quiet as Hughes had expected it to be. St. Leon showed up on time. The Ranger stepped from the shadows.

"Well, if it's not old Diamond Dick," Hughes said. "How are you taking to working with a pickax instead of a pistol?"

St. Leon smiled. "Work's work, however you do it. But I do miss riding with you boys. I guess you're here to put a stop to this thievin' business."

"I see you haven't stopped thinking like a Ranger," Hughes replied. "What can you tell me?"

St. Leon took a cigar from his vest, bit off the end, and reached in his pocket for a match.

"Some of the boys in the mine figure they're not getting paid enough in wages, so they're helping themselves to the highest grade ore," St. Leon said. "They salt the ore away in a shaft they don't use anymore. Every week or so, other members of the gang come up from Mexico with burros and pack the ore across the river. They've been doing it so long, they don't think they're going to get found out, John."

The Ranger listened to St. Leon's report, interrupting every once in a while to ask a question.

"I've got a notion how we can put these thieves out of business, but I'm going to need your help, Dick," Hughes said.

"Been mighty dull around here lately, John. What can I do to help?"

Coyotes yelped in the distance as Hughes and the ex-Ranger parleyed for another couple of hours in the dark cemetery overlooking the bustling mining town. In the morning, Hughes would have another visit with the mine superintendent.

*　　*　　*　　*　　*

Not long after his talk with Ranger Hughes, St. Leon was called into the front office at the mine and was fired on the spot. The ex-Ranger threw a fit.

"Fire me, will you? I've got half a mind to get me some dynamite and put this miserable mine out of business for good!"

St. Leon, red-faced and cursing, marched out of the mine office and continued his performance outside. Wide-eyed miners began gathering around him as he continued to rant and rave about being fired.

"By God, if I can't work like an honest man, I believe I'll have me a drink," he said and strode purposefully to the nearest saloon, followed by a throng of miners.

St. Leon held forth noisily in the bar, appearing to knock down drink after drink. More and more miners came to see the show and have a drink themselves. Before long, they were beginning to agree with St. Leon that he had been unjustly fired from the mine.

From a discreet distance, Ranger Hughes watched all the commotion. St. Leon's prearranged "firing" was all part of the Ranger's plan, and so was the play-acting in the bar. In fact, Hughes was beginning to worry that St. Leon was doing too good of a job in his effort to convince the miners — and the thieves — he had been wronged by the mine owners. The ex-Ranger had the miners so stirred up, Hughes feared they might mob the mine.

Just in time, St. Leon stormed out of the bar announcing he was going to Mexico.

As Hughes had expected, the ex-Ranger's big show had greatly impressed the miners, including the thieves. St. Leon had shown such contempt for the mine owners that the bandits invited him to join their gang.

Hughes knew it would only be a matter of time before St. Leon learned when and where the next burro caravan of stolen ore would be crossing the Rio Grande. The Ranger left Shafter to report these latest developments to Captain Jones. He was going to be needing some help.

The captain ordered Ranger Lon Oden to return with Hughes to Shafter. When they got back to the remote mining town, Oden took a hotel room and lay low. Hughes did not want anyone to know there were now two Rangers in town.

Meanwhile, Hughes met with St. Leon and learned a pack train would be moving out of Mexico that night to pick up the latest stash of hidden silver ore at the mine.

That night, Hughes and Ranger Oden slipped up to the abandoned mine entrance where the stolen ore had been concealed. They picked a hiding place with a good view behind some boulders and settled down to wait for the bandits.

The later it got, the colder it got. The two Rangers shivered in the chilly mountain air.

"By golly, John, if we wait much longer, I believe my hands will be frozen to my gun barrel," Oden whispered through chattering teeth.

"Dick said they would be here tonight and I believe him," Hughes said. "The state doesn't pay us to be comfortable, but I'm as cold as you are. I'd give all the silver in Shafter right now for a hot cup of coffee!"

For another hour, the two Rangers suffered in silence.

"Lon, I believe I hear something," Hughes whispered, his words turning to steam from the cold.

The two Rangers listened. Sure enough, they could hear the creak of saddle leather and the jingle of bits and chains. The pack train was coming, just as St. Leon had said.

Finally, a burro started coming up the trail beneath the Rangers. Then another and another. In all, six burros and four men were slowly moving up the trail in the darkness.

Hughes squinted to make out the faces of the men. St. Leon was one of them.

As the Rangers continued to watch, the men stopped

the burros at the mouth of the old tunnel. Three of them went inside, leaving St. Leon outside to watch the burros.

Directly, the men returned carrying bags that Hughes and Oden knew were full of stolen silver ore. They loaded the first burro and went back into the mine.

"That's all we needed to see," Hughes whispered to Ranger Oden.

Corporal Hughes stood up with his Winchester on his shoulder. Oden popped up next to him, his rifle also at the ready.

"Throw up your hands . . . Texas Rangers!" Hughes yelled.

The ore thieves froze for an instant and dropped the heavy sacks they had been toting. But their hands went down, not up.

Blazes of orange came out the ends of their pistols as they blasted away in the direction of Hughes' voice. They could not see the Rangers in the darkness, but they were shooting in the right area. A bullet zipped past Hughes' ear as the two Rangers started shooting back.

St. Leon levered his Winchester and joined the fight in behalf of the Rangers. In the withering crossfire, two of the badmen went down. The third thief ducked into the tunnel as St. Leon ran around to join the two Rangers.

"Nice work, Dick," Hughes told the former Ranger. "Now all we've got to do is get that last fellow out of that tunnel. His cover is too good for us to rush him. We may just have to wait him out."

Hughes figured he would try the easy way first, though.

"Come out with your hands up and you won't be harmed!" he yelled.

The man in the tunnel let loose with a volley of curses but made no offer to surrender.

Hughes then appealed to the man's sense of honor. One of the downed outlaws was still alive, moaning in pain. "If you care anything about your friend there, surrender so we can give him water," the Ranger shouted.

The outlaw said nothing.

"I can't leave that poor devil out there suffering," Hughes told the other two men.

The Ranger corporal dropped down and began crawling toward the wounded outlaw, hoping to get him out of the line of fire and do whatever he could for him. But the Ranger was still several yards away from the man when a bullet from the tunnel splatted into the ground not far from his head.

Oden and St. Leon began firing into the tunnel and Hughes hurried back to cover.

"You may as well come on out," St. Leon yelled to the outlaw. "We're not leaving until we have you."

The only reply was a curse and a shot fired in St. Leon's direction.

"Let's see if we can't get him to waste some more bullets," Oden said. "If he runs out of ammunition, we can take him easy."

Hughes thought it over. The outlaw was not going anywhere. Despite the cold, they would just wait him out. It was cold in the tunnel too.

The outlaw must have reckoned he had a better chance while it was still dark.

Hughes saw St. Leon tense up and raise his rifle.

"Drop your gun!" the former Ranger shouted.

A single .30-.30 blast echoed against the surrounding rocks and St. Leon ran toward the tunnel, followed by the two Rangers.

The outlaw had tried to slip out of the tunnel and St. Leon had seen him. His shot had felled the outlaw, who was still gripping his rifle in death. Hughes looked down at the fallen outlaw and then turned to St. Leon.

"Dick, you've done a fine job, but I guess you know that if you stay around Shafter, word will get around that you fell in with these fellows just to help out the Rangers. Your life won't be worth an empty .30-.30 shell. You'd better leave now."

"You're right as rain, John, but I had sure taken a

liking to this country. I'll ride on, at least until things cool down."

*   *   *   *   *

The following day, Hughes buried the unclaimed bodies of the three outlaws on a mountaintop near the trail they had used to carry the stolen silver ore to Mexico. He collected a reward offered by the mining company and saw that most of it went to St. Leon.

Hughes did not forget the outlaw he had been trailing in New Mexico when Captain Jones had ordered him back to Texas to handle the problem at Shafter. Sometime later, the Ranger got word that Geronimo Parra was in prison in New Mexico. Working with Pat Garrett, the New Mexican lawman who had gained fame for gunning down Billy the Kid, Hughes arranged a trade. The Ranger tracked down a Texas man wanted in New Mexico and handed him over to Garrett in exchange for Parra, who was eventually hanged.

When it was safe for "Diamond Dick" St. Leon to return to the Big Bend country, he worked with Hughes and his Rangers in a second undercover operation. By this time Hughes had risen to captain, and in appreciation for St. Leon's dedicated work he hired him back on as a Texas Ranger.

*   *   *   *   *

On June 30, 1893, Captain Jones was killed in a gun battle along the Rio Grande near El Paso. Hughes, by then a sergeant, was promoted to captain of Company D. He continued his service with the Rangers until his retirement in 1915. Shortly before Hughes' retirement, Western writer Zane Grey came to Texas and rode with Hughes and his men to gather material for his classic novel, *The Lone Star Ranger*. Grey dedicated the book to Hughes and his men. Years later, Grey's action-packed novel became the inspiration behind the creation of one of America's better known fictional characters: the Lone Ranger.

By the turn of the century, the Rangers of the Frontier Battalion had done their duty so well that they had practically worked their way out of a job. The Indians were long gone, and though crime had not ended, Texas was clearly a more peaceful place than it had been in the 1870s.

On top of that, an opinion by the Texas attorney general held that the law creating the Frontier Battalion was defective: only the officers, not Ranger privates, had the power to make arrests. Of course, Rangers had made thousands of arrests in the quarter-century history of the Frontier Battalion, including 579 the year before. But with the legal opinion, the Rangers were practically powerless to enforce the law.

The Frontier Battalion was reduced to a skeleton force until July 8, 1901, when the legislature passed a new law creating four companies of Rangers. Each Ranger, regardless of rank, had the power to make arrests.

7

Trailing *Tequileros*

Texas — and the Texas Rangers — were changing. Rangers still patrolled the border country on horseback, but they also used the newfangled car. The automobile, thanks to the development of the gasoline engine and Henry Ford's assembly line, was replacing the horse and buggy as the main way of getting around in Texas and across the nation. Horseless carriages needed gasoline, not oats. The growing world demand for oil and petroleum products brought a new law-enforcement problem for the Texas Rangers.

During World War I, the large Ranger force had been strengthened by another 400 Special Rangers appointed by the governor. Rangers watched the border, looking for German spies and draft dodgers. In 1919, after the war, the Texas legislature decided to cut back on the number of Rangers. The force was reduced to four companies of fifteen men, along with a sergeant and a captain. A headquarters company of six Rangers in Austin under a senior captain also was authorized.

Texas' first oil gusher had blown in at Spindletop,

near Beaumont in Southeast Texas, on January 10, 1901. In little more than a week, the discovery well produced 800,000 barrels of oil. This was the beginning of Texas' oil industry, though the real boom did not come until after the fighting ended in Europe in 1918 and the world was at peace.

The days ahead, however, would prove anything but peaceful for the Texas Rangers.

Texas' economy exploded as spectacularly as the fireballs that shot up from burning storage tanks or blown-out wells. Vast fortunes were quickly made and sometimes as quickly lost by land speculators and wildcatters.

Starting in 1901 and continuing through the early 1930s, oil exploration moved from the upper Texas coast to Northwest Texas, to West Texas, to Central Texas, and finally, to East Texas. Boom towns sprang up at each new oil field. Wooden oil derricks covered once open countryside like a field of giant rain lilies after a spring thunderstorm. Places like Borger, Burkburnett, Desdemona, Mexia, Ranger, and Kilgore boomed.

Wallowing in oil and money, these boom towns quickly attracted lawless elements intent on enjoying their share of the action — and preferably, someone else's share. When crime could no longer be controlled by local officers, the Texas Rangers were sent in to restore order.

Another problem facing the Rangers was national prohibition. Beginning on January 17, 1920, federal law made it illegal to manufacture, sell, or transport intoxicating liquors. The law was intended to rid the country of the devastating problems of alcohol abuse. Instead, it brought more crime and a new headache for the Rangers.

Alcohol was still available in Mexico and other foreign countries, and illegal trafficking of liquor was soon a thriving business. Texas was practically invaded by Mexican smugglers, who moved loads of liquor, predominantly tequila, across the border into South Texas. The

Texas Rangers worked with federal officers to capture these smugglers and destroy their illegal product.

With prohibition and the oil-boom problems, the decade of the twenties was a busy time for the Rangers. The end of the decade marked the end of the Rangers' near total reliance on the horse and the beginning of state law enforcement by Rangers who did their traveling by automobile.

*   *   *   *   *

Leroy Adolph was the youngest reporter on the *San Antonio Express*. He sat at his battered Remington upright typewriter, staring at the blank piece of copy paper he had rolled in a half-hour before. Elsewhere in the newsroom, reporters hammered away on their typewriters, yanking out each page as they finished it and yelling "Copy!" That one-word order sent the copy boy scrambling to pick up the reporter's latest "take" and hustle it over to the city desk.

But Leroy was not fighting a deadline. He was having enough trouble trying to think of something interesting to write about that day's meeting of the Alamo City Businessmen's Club. For what seemed like the dozenth time, he looked down at the notes he had scribbled on a folded piece of copy paper. His story, if he could get it written, was for the Sunday paper. Adolph wanted to write a big story about something really important, but he knew his city editor was not likely to give that kind of story to someone who had barely turned eighteen.

"Adolph! Get over here." The voice boomed across the newsroom, coming from the cloud of gray cigar smoke hovering over the city desk. Inside the haze was City Editor Charlie "Chophouse" Welch. He never called his reporters by their first names.

Leroy got up and walked quickly to the city desk, expecting a chewing out for something.

Welch was a San Antonio legend. Like most good editors, he had worked himself up from cub reporter, spending a lot of time at the police station covering crime news before he got the city desk job.

"What are you working on?" Chophouse asked, dispensing with any pleasantries.

"You sent me to cover the men's business club," Leroy said. "I'm stuck for a good lead."

Welch acted like he hadn't even heard him.

"Forget it. I don't much care what those booster boys do. I've got something else for you. Ever hear of Capt. Will Wright?"

Leroy shook his head.

"Well, Will Wright is probably the most respected Ranger in Texas. He was chasing outlaws before you were born. These days he's making life hard on liquor smugglers down along the border. I want a full story on the captain and his men, with pictures."

Leroy opened his mouth to ask a question, but Welch did not wait to hear it.

"I've known Captain Wright since I covered a hanging he presided over in Floresville more than twenty years ago. If he gives you any trouble about tagging along with him for a spell, just tell 'im I sent you."

Welch took a long, reflective puff on his cigar.

"Here's a voucher for $8 to cover your expenses. If you've got any money left over when you get back to town, turn it back in to Accounting. You'll find the captain in Laredo. The train leaves at two o'clock."

Leroy felt that he ought to salute or something.

"Thanks for the assignment, Chophouse," he said.

Welch smiled. "Have you ever ridden a horse, Adolph?"

"No, but I can drive an automobile."

Welch seemed to think that was awfully funny.

"In that case, you better hold your appreciation until you get back with the story. Then you can thank me if you want."

*　　*　　*　　*　　*

As the train headed south, Leroy alternated between reading the competition newspaper, the *Light,* and watching the telegraph poles and mesquite trees flash by the train window. Since he had to be at work by 6:00 every morning, he had been awake since before sunup. He leaned back and closed his eyes.

"Next stop, Laredo!" the conductor shouted, waking Leroy.

Union Station in San Antonio was a constant whirl of activity, but the pace was slower on the border. Leroy got directions from the station agent and walked to the sheriff's office at the courthouse.

From the sheriff, he learned Captain Wright and his men had a camp on the Los Ojuelos Ranch about forty miles downriver.

"Can I get there by streetcar?" Leroy asked.

The sheriff laughed. "Son, this ain't San Antonio," he explained. "The whole reason the Rangers are out there is because it's out in the middle of nowhere. It's near where the smugglers like to cross over into Texas. Only way out there is by horse or motorcar."

The sheriff pushed his hat back and thought for a moment.

"The captain sends his driver in for grub every week or so," he said. "Whenever he needs to wire headquarters in Austin, a Ranger will come in with a message and see if any orders have arrived from Austin. Trouble is, we never know for sure when a Ranger will show up here in town."

What sounded like a shot made the sheriff jump and reach instinctively for his pistol as he ran to the window.

"Was that a shot, sheriff?" Leroy asked, fishing for his pencil and notepaper.

"Could be that or . . . well, you're in luck, son," the sheriff said as he holstered his pistol. "Wasn't a gun going off. Just the Ranger's T Model truck a backfiring. That's Bob Winters, young fellow Captain Wright pays to be his driver. If you want a ride out to Los Ojuelos, you

71

best get yourself out there and make Bob's acquaintance."

*　　*　　*　　*　　*

A couple of hours later, Leroy and Bob were on their way back to Captain Wright's camp.

"Cap doesn't have much use for reporters," Bob told Leroy, just to make conversation. "One time Cap asked a newspaper photographer real polite like not to take no pictures. The fellow went ahead and snapped the shutter. Next thing I knew, one of the boys' pistols went off accidentally. The bullet happened to shoot the camera right out of the old boy's hands. Bring your camera along?"

After bouncing along for several hours down the two-rut road, Leroy finally saw a collection of white buildings in the distance. In the setting sun, the stone houses took on a golden glow.

"This here's Los Ojuelos," Bob said. "Means little springs in Spanish. Only spring between the Rio Grande and the Nueces. Ain't much of a place — just a few houses, a church, a school, a blacksmith, a store and a little cafe out here in the middle of the chaparral. We've been camping at a house across from the eating place."

Bob stopped the truck outside the headquarters of Company D, Texas Rangers. Out back was a fair-sized corral, but only one horse.

"Don't look like Cap's back yet," Bob said. "The boys be expecting some grub when they get in. We better get started. Grab that bag of flour."

The house had two big rooms. One was where the Rangers bunked. The other was a combination kitchen and dining room. A long wooden table with benches on either side filled the middle of the room. Over in a corner was a wood-burning cookstove.

"When you get the truck empty, haul us in some wood," Bob said. "Woodpile's out back. I'll get started on the biscuits."

The pot of beans left over from breakfast, freshened

72

with some onion slices and an apple, was simmering on the stove and the flour-dusted biscuits were browning when Leroy heard riders. He went out on the porch and saw a column of horsemen approaching in the twilight.

Leroy blinked his eyes. In the lead was a man who was practically a dead ringer for Teddy Roosevelt, the former president. But Leroy knew Roosevelt was not in South Texas. The man on the dark horse had a droopy mustache and round wire glasses just like those favored by Roosevelt. A rifle scabbard hung from the man's saddle and a big six-shooter rode on his hip.

Behind this man was the toughest-looking group of men Leroy had ever seen. They were different sizes and wore different clothes, but they all had one thing in common: they were covered in dust.

The column stopped in front of the house.

"You boys see to your horses," the leader shouted, walking his horse toward the house.

The man dismounted, took his hat off to shake off some of the dust, and walked up to the porch.

"I'm Captain Wright," he said. "You have some business being on our porch?"

"Yes, sir," Leroy replied. "I'm a representative of the *San Antonio Express*. I'm here to do a story on you and your Rangers."

Wright stared at the young reporter for a moment before extending his hand. He was more wary of a reporter than a brush country bandit, but too polite not to shake.

"I don't have much to say to reporters," he said. "They write fanciful stories on the Rangers, making us look like a bunch of moving picture cowboys. My boys just do their job. It's a mighty risky one at that."

Wright seemed reserved, but beneath that, Leroy sensed a man with a big heart and a sense of humor. Leroy also knew he had not made any progress with the Ranger captain. He decided to play his ace.

"Chophouse Welch sent me to talk to you," he said.

"Chophouse Welch!" Wright roared. "You mean nobody's killed him yet? He was one reporter I respected. He came down for a big hanging we had when I was a deputy sheriff in Wilson County, back in '97. I dern near fell through the trap myself and Welch had the good grace not to put that in his write-up. 'Course, maybe he didn't see it. Come around back while I tend to old Jack here and we'll talk some more."

*   *   *   *   *

In the end, Leroy figured the captain agreed to the story because he felt sorry for him. The captain knew as well as Leroy did what the cub reporter would face if he went back to San Antonio without a story.

"We'll head out again at daybreak," the captain finally said. "Can you ride a horse?"

Leroy considered running a bluff, but there was something about the captain's intent gaze that told him better men had tried to lie to Will Wright and had failed.

"No, sir, I've never had occasion to learn to ride a horse. I sure can drive a car, though."

Wright broke into a Teddy Roosevelt grin. "I think Old Widowmaker will suit you just fine. He's real gentle. Now let's get some supper."

*   *   *   *   *

The first thing Leroy learned about the Rangers was that they ate heartily. The *frijoles* and biscuits were washed down with boiled coffee. Supper was rounded out with stewed wild plums, collected from the surrounding brush.

"What will we be doing tomorrow, Captain?" Leroy asked, digging into his vest for his pencil.

"Same thing we've been doing most days since prohibition went in," the captain replied. "The smugglers — we call 'em *tequileros* — are about to run us ragged. They smuggle tequila across the Rio Grande in pack trains and move the liquor about halfway between here and San Antonio. Then the bootlegger boys pick up the load and carry the stuff on up farther north. But some of these smugglers don't make it. Those are the ones we run up on."

"What do you do when you find them?" Leroy asked, busily taking notes.

"We tell 'em to stick up their hands and surrender, *rindarse* in Spanish. Those that seem to need too much time to think about it are quickly reminded it's a mighty dangerous business they're in. After the shooting stops, we bust up the tequila bottles and collect their pack horses. If we're close enough and there's enough light left, we come on back to camp here. If not, we'll make camp where we are and have some supper. Next day we start cutting for sign again."

Leroy wrote all that down. "What does 'cutting for sign' mean?" he asked.

"We look for fresh trails," the captain said. "These *tequileros* are not stupid. They know this side of the river as well as their side. And they know how to move through this country very skillfully."

"Don't they know you Rangers are out in the brush looking for them?" Leroy asked.

"Sure they do. But there's an awful lot of money in it for them if they succeed in getting a load across," the captain said as he used a piece of biscuit to sop the "pot liquor" at the bottom of his bean bowl.

"These *tequileros* are tough hombres too," the captain continued. "Many of them fought in the revolution down there in Mexico. A lot of them are bandits who have been raiding into Texas since they've been old enough to straddle a horse and shoot a rifle. We've had some innocent ranchers killed just because they accidentally crossed their path. Our job is to stop the flow of liquor into Texas and discourage these bandits from crossing the Rio Grande."

*   *   *   *   *

75

Leroy awoke to the clanging of a cookspoon against the inside of a big pan.

"Rise and shine, boys," Bob shouted, banging the pan. "Coffee's boiling."

"Where's my pistol?" one of the Rangers asked. "Too much racket in here for a man to sleep."

The first thing Leroy realized was that he was not in San Antonio. The next thing he noticed was that the only light outside was coming from the moon.

"Good morning, Leroy," the captain said. "Let's go get your horse saddled up. Then we'll eat. Seeing to your horse first thing in the morning is more important out here in the brush than a full belly."

After a breakfast of refried beans, tortillas, and black coffee, the Rangers moved out. The captain, riding Jack, was in the lead. Next to him was Leroy on Old Widowmaker, who was much more docile than his name suggested.

"Widowmaker used to have a wild streak in him, but age has gentled him up," the captain explained. "Just go easy on them reins. He knows what to do."

They rode all morning through the brush. All they saw were cattle and an occasional startled deer crashing through the mesquite.

"Rangering ain't all shoot 'em ups," the captain offered. "It's hours in the saddle away from home, prickly pear thorns festering in your hide, and missed sleep and missed meals. But it's a day's work. I'd rather be out here on a good horse than anything else I can think of."

*   *   *   *   *

By the second day of the scout, Leroy was having to stand in his stirrups. Even thinking about sitting down hurt.

"I've got some ointment that'll help the saddle sores," the captain said when he noticed Leroy's pained look. "It works on men and horses."

Leroy, aside from his saddle sores, was beginning to

worry nothing would happen on the scout. "Chophouse" expected a story pretty soon, and though he had learned some interesting particulars about Rangers and smugglers, there was no real news to report.

Suddenly, the captain reined in Jack and dismounted.

"Well, well," he said. "Looks like a bunch of riders crossed this trail not long back. We may have some business, boys."

They followed the trail until dusk.

"Yonder's where they spent last night," the captain said, pointing to a pile of ashes and blackened wood. Left behind were several empty tequila bottles and a scattering of empty cans punctured with bullet holes. "Looks like they got in a little shooting practice. Maybe they're such good shots they figure they don't need to cover their trail."

*   *   *   *   *

That night, they made a cold camp — no fire and only tortillas to eat. And like every morning since the scout began, they were up before dawn.

"I can't figure why they're leaving such an easy trail," one of the Rangers told the captain. "You reckon they're trying to draw us into an ambush?"

The captain studied on that for a moment. "No, I think they're just being careless. May be sampling a little too much of their own product."

The Rangers rode all day. Leroy was barely able to stay in the saddle. Then he saw the captain rein in Jack.

"Look there. An empty tequila bottle. It'll be a wonder if they have anything left for us to seize when we catch up to 'em." The captain dismounted and started tugging on the rolled tarp behind his saddle. As Leroy watched, he pulled out a short, double-barreled shotgun.

"Here, son, I want you to carry this," the captain told Leroy. "It's a ten-gauge, loaded with buckshot. If we get into a tight spot you might be needing this. All you've got to do is click back the hammers and pull one trigger and then the other. Be careful you don't pull both triggers at once or you'll clear a hole in the brush big enough for us to drive a wagon through."

Leroy hefted the gun.

"Captain, I'm here to write a story, not shoot anybody."

The captain flashed his Roosevelt grin again.

"I don't expect you'll need it, but if you do, it'll come in mighty handy. Boys, let's go pay a little social call."

In thirty minutes, Leroy smelled smoke.

The captain held up his hand and the column stopped.

"I 'spect we're smelling their campfire," he said in a loud whisper. "Let's ease on up and invite ourselves for supper."

The Rangers dismounted and tied their horses. From here on, Leroy realized with relief, the traveling would be by foot.

The brush was so thick the Rangers were practically on top of the *tequilero* camp before they spotted it. The smugglers had the saddles off their horses and their pack animals unloaded. The liquor boxes were stacked in a big pile. One case had been broken open and the men were passing a bottle around.

"John, you and Don come with me and Leroy," the captain said. "You other boys circle around to the side."

Leroy went back to his horse and pulled his camera from his saddlebag.

The captain walked up. "Son, you'd best take that scattergun right now. You can snap all the pictures you want when we're finished. I don't want anyone getting hurt, unless it's one of them smugglers."

Leroy knew Captain Wright was not a man to argue with. He untied the shotgun from his saddle and followed the captain. The shotgun felt cold and heavy in his hands.

Satisfied the other Rangers were in position, the captain levered a shell into his .30-.30. Slowly they moved through the brush toward the smugglers' camp.

"Rindarse!" the captain shouted, breaking into the clearing.

The drunken smugglers were taken completely by surprise, but they were not too full of tequila to keep them from shooting.

The captain's command to surrender was answered by a flurry of gunshots. What sounded like a mad bee zipped past Leroy's left ear.

"Get down, son," Wright shouted, cutting loose with his Winchester.

Leroy counted six smugglers. Four fell in a hail of Ranger fire. The fifth ran into the brush and the sixth ducked behind the stack of tequila crates and opened up with his rifle.

Suddenly, the Ranger next to Leroy grabbed his leg and went down.

The captain and the other men were firing from prone positions at the tequila boxes.

Another bullet splatted against a mesquite trunk about eight inches from Leroy's head.

"He's shooting at me!" Leroy shouted.

Leroy pulled back both hammers of the shotgun, pointed it toward the stack of boxes, and stood into a crouch.

"Watch out, boy!" the captain shouted as Leroy pulled both triggers.

*　*　*　*　*

The next thing Leroy knew, he was on his back, looking up at the orange sky of sunset. Then he realized the shooting had stopped and that the captain and the other Rangers were standing over him, laughing.

"I told you to be careful about pulling both triggers at once," the captain said with a smile. "On the other hand, when that double load of buckshot hit those tequila crates, that fellow who'd been doing most of the shooting didn't have much cover left. Threw his hands up and surrendered, real mannerly. The last one got away, but a couple of the boys went after him. The other four won't be doing any more smuggling."

Leroy stood and dusted himself off.

"I'm sorry, I didn't mean to shoot," Leroy stammered. "But he nearly killed me."

The captain picked up the shotgun.

"I'll take care of this," he said. "You go get your camera. I hope you've got a flashgun. You're losing light fast."

*　　*　　*　　*　　*

"Chophouse" Welch flipped through the stack of photographs, took a long drag on his cigar, and looked up at Leroy.

"Can you type standing up?" he laughed. "Write your story as long as you want and you better get started. I'm running it on page one."

Leroy walked slowly back to his desk, pushed back his chair, rolled a piece of paper in his typewriter, and started pounding the keys with two fingers.

*　　*　　*　　*　　*

Prohibition, the "noble experiment," ended one minute after midnight on September 15, 1933. The same year, Captain Wright ended his long career as a Texas Ranger. He moved back to Wilson County, where he had grown up, and lived there until his death in 1942. Rangers and other lawmen came from all over Texas to attend his funeral. They came in cars. The days of the horseback Rangers were over.

8

"I'm Frank Hamer"

In the early 1930s, Texas and the rest of the nation were suffering through the depths of history's worst financial Depression. Banks were failing and millions of men and women were out of work and were hungry. As if the nation did not have enough to worry about, crime was widespread. Nationwide, 12,000 murders were reported in 1933. In a five-year period beginning in 1928, more than 4,000 murder cases were prosecuted in Texas. Many more slayings went unsolved. Kidnappings and bank robberies plagued law enforcement across the nation, and Texas was no exception. The Texas Rangers had plenty of business.

The bank robbery situation was so bad in Texas that the Texas Bankers Association offered a $5,000 reward for bank robbers — dead or alive. Unfortunately, some crooks saw the reward as just one more way to make money. A sudden upswing in dead bank robbers looked suspicious to Texas Ranger Capt. Frank Hamer, who started looking into some of the cases. He found what he suspected. Corrupt lawmen and other supposedly upstanding citizens were setting up phony bank robberies and killing innocent people to be able to claim the reward. Hamer exposed the scheme by outlining it to the press. The banking association changed its policy and made the reward for live robbers only. That problem ended.

Texas had still another worry. Texas Rangers were picked by the adjutant general, who was appointed by the governor. A governor also could appoint Rangers directly. The result was a highly political Ranger force. Many good men served in the Rangers, but as governors changed, Rangers came and went. The system was ripe for abuse.

In 1933, Miriam Ferguson was elected as Texas' first woman governor. She was the wife of Jim Ferguson, who had a less honorable distinction. He had been the first Texas governor to be impeached (removed from office for corruption), in 1917. When Mrs. Ferguson was sworn into office, Captain Hamer and forty other honest Rangers resigned.

Under Mrs. Ferguson, Ranger jobs were particularly easy to get. The governor also appointed roughly 2,300 Special Rangers, some of them ex-convicts. The early 1930s were the darkest days of the Rangers. But for Frank Hamer, his most challenging assignment lay ahead.

*   *   *   *   *

A dense fog hovered over the Trinity River bottom as the prisoners marched toward the cotton fields early on the morning of January 16, 1934. Hoes to their shoulders, the line of men in prison whites moved toward their long day's work under the watchful eyes of two prison guards. Nearby was the narrow highway that passed next to the Eastham Prison Farm.

As the prisoners continued their familiar daily march, convict Joe Palmer looked toward a culvert near the woodyard. He knew what he was looking for. Careful

to make his moves while the guards were looking elsewhere, Palmer bent down quickly at the culvert and
came up with a .45-caliber automatic pistol. The heavy
weapon was deathly cool to the touch.

The convict quickly checked to make sure a shell had
already been jacked into the chamber. Satisfied the pistol
was ready for instant action, the convict swung around
and pointed the powerful handgun at the guards.

"This is a break! Don't you guards make a move, or
we'll let you have it!"

The guards had no time to react.

Another convict, Raymond Hamilton, a robber and
killer whose habits were listed as "tempermental" in
prison records, reached into the culvert and pulled out
another .45. So far, everything was going as planned.

Tires screeched as a dark Ford roared down the highway, stopping next to the armed prisoners. The guards
had time to notice the car was driven by a young man
wearing a snapbrim hat. Next to him sat an attractive
blonde. Another man also was in the car.

But there was no more time for study. Gunfire exploded the early-morning quiet.

In a matter of seconds, nearly 100 rounds had been
fired. One of the guards lay dead.

Hamilton, Palmer, and two other prisoners jumped
into the big Ford and sped away, leaving the other prisoners behind. Two of the most-wanted outlaws in the
Southwest, Clyde Barrow, Jr., and Bonnie Parker, had
just sprung their old buddy, Raymond Hamilton, from
prison. Along for the ride were an assortment of other
hoods who did not mind taking a chance at freedom, even
though they did not personally know the young couple
who had made it possible. But even in prison, the con-
victs had all heard of Bonnie and Clyde.

Prison officials soon learned the details of the escape
plot. Not long before the break, a thug named James
Mullin had been released from the Eastham Unit of the

prison. Officials felt he might know something about the break and had him arrested for questioning.

As it turned out, in the short time he had been out, Mullin had been arrested on another charge and was already on his way back to prison. But he did not care for hoeing cotton. The prison administration agreed to see that he served his next sentence in a federal prison, a place considered a country club compared to the Texas prison system. Mullin agreed to talk.

When he was released from prison, Mullin said, he carried a message to Hamilton's brother, Floyd: Ask Clyde Barrow to help break Raymond Hamilton out of prison. The weekend before the escape, Floyd had visited his brother in prison and filled him in on the plans. In the predawn darkness the day before the escape, the two pistols were hidden. Bonnie and Clyde, along with Mullin, would drive up on the prison work party the next morning. The plan had worked perfectly.

*   *   *   *   *

Col. Lee Simmons had spent another restless night, barely able to sleep. As superintendent of the Texas State Prison, it was his job to get the escapees back behind bars. And now that Ray Hamilton had been in on the killing of a prison guard, he could be executed if convicted of the murder. Simmons wanted Bonnie and Clyde too. Of course, so did every peace officer in Texas.

Unable to sleep, Simmons got out of bed and went to another room where he could turn on a light and not disturb his wife. He had an idea and he was thinking it through. Hours later, he smiled and headed back to bed to catch a few hours' sleep before the alarm clock would start clanging. He believed his idea just might work.

*   *   *   *   *

Simmons' first step was to appear before the prison board. The state's budget was tight as Texas continued to struggle through the Depression. But Simmons wanted approval to create a new position: special investigator for the Texas Prison System. The prison board would have to give its blessing, and the governor would have to give final approval.

Simmons told the board he wanted to hire a veteran manhunter, someone he could depend on to keep going until he captured Bonnie and Clyde. The board asked who Simmons had in mind. He told them he was still thinking about that and would let them know when he made a decision.

The prison superintendent knew one thing. He wanted his special investigator to come from the ranks of the Texas Rangers, preferably a captain, a man with a proven crime-fighting record. One man who met all the requirements Simmons had in mind was former Ranger Capt. Frank Hamer.

Hamer bore the scars of many a bullet from men who foolishly had thought they could outshoot him. He had been a Ranger for almost thirty years and had survived at least fifty gunfights. When he had first joined the force, Rangers still did most of their scouting on horseback. But Hamer had adapted to the times and was as comfortable behind the wheel of a powerful sedan as he was on the back of a horse in the brush country.

Hamer did not talk much, but he got results. He was known as the most fearless, effective Ranger of his generation. Hamer also believed in playing it straight. He would not tolerate official crookedness, or even the taint of it. That was why Hamer had resigned his Ranger commission when Miriam Ferguson became governor.

Simmons, of course, knew how Hamer felt about the Fergusons and feared they might feel the same way about Hamer. Knowing he had to handle it carefully, he went to see the governor.

The prison director met Governor Ferguson and her husband Jim in the governor's capitol office.

"As you know, Governor, we lost a guard in the escape pulled by Bonnie and Clyde," Simmons began.

"Those two have now been involved in the killing of at least ten people and no telling how many hijackings. We've got to stop them."

The Fergusons were well aware of the crime wave triggered by the deadly young couple. The Texas Rangers were already on the case and a $1,000 reward had been posted by the legislature for Clyde Barrow, dead or alive. The reward for Raymond Hamilton was $500.

"I want to hire a special investigator, someone whose only job will be to catch Bonnie and Clyde and Raymond Hamilton if he's still with them," Simmons said. "The Rangers still have other cases to worry about and cannot concentrate fully on Bonnie and Clyde. But I want someone who represents the best of the Rangers — Frank Hamer. Any objections?"

Governor Ferguson responded immediately. "Frank is all right with us," the governor said. "We don't hold anything against him."

Simmons had more to his plan.

Hamer had a lot of underworld connections, Simmons told the governor and her husband. He knew from years of experience that, true to the old saying, there was no honor among thieves. It might take some of Barrow's former cronies to help catch him, and Hamer was the man who could put it all together.

"I might want to put somebody on the ground," Simmons told the governor. He explained he might want to promise someone a pardon in exchange for information leading to the capture of Bonnie and Clyde. "Is that all right with you, Governor?"

"Yes, that is all right with me,'" she said.

*   *   *   *   *

Simmons' next visit was to Frank Hamer, who was doing security work for an oil company in Houston.

"Frank, you know what the Barrow gang has been up to. They're driving all over creation in a fast Ford, robbing and killing. Now they've sprung Hamilton."

"I've seen the papers," Hamer said.

Simmons laid out his plan to the former Ranger.

"You will be completely in charge and I'll back you to the limit," Simmons said.

Simmons knew if Hamer took the job, it would mean a cut in pay for him. When he had left the Rangers, the oil company had quickly hired him at $500 a month, a fine salary. The State could pay Hamer only $180 a month.

But Simmons had known Hamer for three decades. He felt that the chance to rid Texas of a couple of cold-blooded killers would mean more to Hamer than money.

The big former Ranger captain tilted back his black hat and looked at Simmons.

"How long do you think it will take to do the job?"

*   *   *   *   *

The meeting between Simmons and Hamer was on February 1, 1934. Nine days later, after closing up loose business ends and seeing to his family, Hamer went on the trail of Bonnie and Clyde. He had equipped himself with a Ford V8, the same fast car favored by the outlaws he was after.

During his years as a Ranger, Hamer had built a reputation for an almost uncanny ability to hunt wanted men. He pursued them with the thought and patience of a skillful game hunter. Hamer knew how to "cut sign," a process of trailing someone by looking for broken twigs, bent stems of grass, rocks kicked out of place. But there was more to following a trail than that. Knowing the habits of the quarry was as important as looking for tracks. Hamer's first step, then, was to learn as much as possible about Barrow and his gun-toting female companion, Bonnie Parker.

Barrow was born in the North Texas community of Teleco, in Ellis County, on March 24, 1909. His father was an illiterate farm hand. Barrow went to school for a while, but dropped out and quickly took up with a gang of automobile thieves and robbers. By 1926, Barrow had been arrested, though he did not go to prison until 1930.

Bonnie Parker was born in the West Texas town of Rowena, northeast of San Angelo, on October 1, 1910. By the late twenties, the family had moved to Dallas. That's where Bonnie met Clyde in January 1930. They fell in love, but a month later Barrow was arrested. Early in March, the love-struck Bonnie smuggled a pistol into the jail and Clyde escaped. His freedom was short-lived. He was recaptured and on April 21, 1930, was sent to the state prison in Huntsville.

Clyde's family immediately started working to get him a pardon, but their efforts were not fast enough for Clyde. Desperate to get out of the hard work in the fields, Clyde got a fellow inmate with an ax to chop off two of his toes. Not long after that, his pardon came through and Clyde was a free man — on crutches. He was released from prison in February 1932, and within a month he and Bonnie were back on the road, robbing mom-and-pop grocery stores, gas stations, and country banks. Their partner in crime was Raymond Hamilton.

One of the first things Hamer realized about the gang was that they tended to travel in a circle from the Dallas area in North Texas to Joplin, Missouri, then to Louisiana and back to Dallas. They varied their routine occasionally, sometimes traveling as far west as New Mexico or north as far as Michigan. Hamer, who was a cowboy before becoming a Ranger, saw the couple as wild horses who would always circle back to their home range. Barrow never stayed in one place very long and was capable of driving as much as a thousand miles in one day.

Hamer traveled the same circle, talking to as many people as he could find who knew Bonnie and Clyde. He wanted to know everything about the couple — what kind of food they ate, their favorite brand of cigarettes, and what label of whiskey they preferred. The determined former Ranger went beyond that — he began to understand how Barrow thought.

Throughout the late winter and early spring of 1934, Hamer pursued the pair. He believed the couple were spending more and more time in Louisiana, where they were not wanted on any charges. Still, Bonnie and Clyde did not seem to be able to stay away from Texas for too long.

*   *   *   *   *

On April 1 — Easter — an elderly farmer sat beneath an oak tree on his place, digesting a big Sunday dinner as cars drove by on the Dallas to Grapevine highway. As he watched the holiday traffic, a new Ford stopped on the side of the road not far from his house. A young couple sat inside, talking and laughing. A whiskey bottle came flying out the car window.

A short time later, two highway patrolmen on motorcycles appeared. They pulled off the highway behind the car and walked toward it, apparently thinking it was stalled and the occupants needed help. With no warning, the man and woman in the car stuck guns out the windows and began shooting at the two officers. The highway patrolmen fell before they could draw their own pistols.

Careful not to be seen, the old farmer slipped up to his fence for a better look. When the shooting stopped, a thin, fair-haired woman stepped out of the car with a sawed-off shotgun in her hands. She calmly walked up to one of the dying officers and fired two more rounds into his head. Then, laughing, she got back into the car, which roared off in a cloud of dust.

Despite an intense search by officers from all over North Texas, the occupants of the car made good their escape. The whiskey bottle tossed from the Ford confirmed what officers had suspected from the moment they drove up on the scene of the double murder: the fingerprints on it belonged to Bonnie and Clyde.

The senseless killing of two young police officers infuriated Hamer. If he had had any doubts before, he knew now that the job he had undertaken was the most important in his law-enforcement career. For some reason, the couple had no regard for human life. They did not always kill the people they robbed, but they had a record of violence that was putting them in the same league with the most notorious gangsters of the era: John Dillinger, Machine Gun Kelly, even Al Capone. Hamer also knew that when he finally caught up with Bonnie and Clyde, they were not likely to surrender meekly.

Hamer stayed on the road constantly. When it was convenient, he took a $2 hotel room, but he often slept in his car, just like the couple he was after. Up to now, he had been working alone. But on April 10, when Hamer called Highway Patrol Chief L. G. Phares with a description of the latest car Barrow was believed to be driving, the chief said he wanted someone on the Highway Patrol to work with him. The man Hamer wanted hired for the job was another former Texas Ranger, B. M. Gault. Hamer and Gault had worked together on many cases, and Hamer trusted him completely. If he ended up in a gunfight with Bonnie and Clyde, it would be a comfort to have another Ranger at his side.

Hamer picked up Gault in Dallas. Two Dallas County sheriff's deputies also joined Hamer.

After the murders in Grapevine, the Barrow gang was next heard from in Oklahoma, where they killed another officer and kidnapped a policeman. From Oklahoma, their trail led back to the piney woods of Louisiana. In Louisiana, Hamer and the other officers found someone willing to provide vital information on the couple's whereabouts.

Hamer knew that even though Bonnie and Clyde were constantly on the run, they still managed to keep in touch with family and friends. Friends received their mail for them and then hid the letters at prearranged spots out in the country. From an informant, Hamer learned where the outlaw couple would be picking up their mail.

In Bienville Parish, Louisiana, Hamer contacted the local sheriff and told him what he had learned: Barrow's "post office" was on a side road about eight miles from the town of Plain Dealing. Mail for Bonnie and Clyde was placed under a board near a large pine stump. Barrow had picked the spot because it was on a knoll, which allowed for a good view down the road in both directions.

"I'm going to furnish him with more news than he's ever received at one time," Hamer told the sheriff. "I'd appreciate your cooperation."

On the night of May 22, Hamer, Gault, the two Dallas deputies, the parish sheriff, and one of his deputies drove to the hiding place and concealed their cars in the pine trees. Hamer had already scouted the area.

"We'll wait for them across the road from Barrow's post office," Hamer explained to the other officers. "This spot gives us the high ground and a better view."

Using pine branches, the officers built a blind to hide behind. Then they settled down to wait for daylight. After the sun came up, a few cars passed along with an occasional logging truck. But no vehicles stopped.

At 9:10 A.M., Hamer and the other officers heard a fast-moving car coming down the road, its motor "singing like a sewing machine." When the car came into view, Hamer saw it was a Ford sedan. As it moved closer to the hidden officers, Hamer could see a man behind the wheel and a woman in the front passenger's seat. The car slowed to a stop right across from the officers.

Hamer's information had been correct. Bonnie and Clyde had come to check their mail.

Clyde kept the car idling as he and Bonnie looked in every direction to make sure no other cars were coming. Both were looking toward the stump when Hamer and the other officers stepped into view.

"Stick 'em up!" Hamer yelled.

Barrow reached for a gun and Bonnie raised her sawed-off shotgun, the same weapon she had used on the two highway patrolmen back in Texas.

Hamer, now standing a few feet in front of the car, did not give Bonnie and Clyde time to fire. He cut loose with his .35-caliber autoloading rifle, which had a twenty-round clip. Bonnie let out a scream like a panther.

Barrow's foot slipped off the clutch and the car, in low gear, moved slowly down the incline of the dirt road. The other officers opened fire, shattering the windows and riddling the Ford with bullet holes. When the car came to a stop, the officers ceased their fire and moved cautiously forward.

Hamer walked in the lead, his .45 semi-automatic thrust forward.

"Be careful, Cap!" Gault yelled. "They may not be dead."

But one look inside the car told Hamer and the other officers that the pursuit of Bonnie and Clyde was over.

The car had been a traveling armory. When Hamer and the other officers checked the contents of the Ford, they found three automatic rifles, two sawed-off shotguns, ten pistols, and 5,000 rounds of ammunition.

Hamer left the other officers at the scene and drove to nearby Arcadia, Louisiana, where he placed a long distance telephone call to Colonel Simmons in Huntsville. After telling the prison director his job had been completed, Hamer called his wife to tell her he was unharmed.

Reporters and news reel camera crews rushed to Arcadia to tell the nation about the end of Bonnie and Clyde. Thousands of curiosity seekers flocked to the site of the shooting to see the bullet-punctured car and look for souvenirs. Grown men fought over empty shells, and people cut pieces of wood from trees looking for spent bullets. The car was towed to town and eventually a promoter got possession of it. He toured the country with it, charging admission for people to be able to see it.

When the tent show came to Austin, Hamer appeared in the crowd. Hamer listened for a while as the promoter tried to sell people on paying to see the car, using Hamer's name frequently in his sales pitch. Finally, the former Ranger captain had had enough.

Hamer jumped up on the stage and confronted the

tent show operator. "I'm Frank Hamer," he said, slapping the man's face. "Don't ever use my name again in public." Hamer stormed off the stage, leaving the promoter rubbing his jaw.

In killing Bonnie and Clyde, Hamer had done what he had to do. In true Texas Ranger spirit, he did not want any recognition for what he had done. Even so, tributes poured in from all over the nation. A telegram from one man pretty well summed up what most people felt after news of what had happened that morning in Louisiana became known: "I feel a damn sight safer driving around at night now thanks to you."

*   *   *   *   *

The violent crime in Texas during the first half of the 1930s made it evident to Texas lawmakers that something had to be done to improve the quality of law enforcement in the state.

On September 25, 1934, the Texas Senate appointed a committee to investigate the crime situation. The committee prepared a report in 1935 that was highly critical of how things stood in Texas. The report, however, contained a suggestion that would radically change the history of the Texas Rangers: A new state agency should be created, one that would merge the Rangers with the Texas Highway Patrol.

Since the 1870s, the Rangers had reported to the Adjutant General's Department. The Highway Patrol, organized in the 1920s as the number of motor vehicles in Texas increased, was part of the Highway Department. The new combination of the Rangers and Highway Patrol would be known as the Texas Department of Public Safety (DPS).

Under the new DPS, which came into being on August 10, 1935, Texas would have thirty-six Rangers. Though smaller than it had been in years, the Ranger force would for the first time have the benefits of formal training in criminology, a modern crime laboratory, state-furnished equipment, and electronic communication.

Some feared that the Rangers, now more than 100 years old, would lose their identity in the new agency. That did not happen. The fame and effectiveness of the Rangers continued to grow. In the late 1940s, a national radio audience thrilled in the exploits of the Rangers while listening to a weekly dramatic show, "Tales of the Texas Rangers." The Texas Rangers were better known and more effective in their crime-fighting than ever before in their history.

9

One-armed Bandits

In the 1950s, the problems facing the Texas Rangers were both old and new. Some types of crime never seem to change. Rangers, as always, were called on for help in solving murders and robberies and other major crimes. But there were fresh challenges.

In a major decision, the United States Supreme Court ruled in 1954 that the old system of "separate but equal" education in the nation was not constitutional. All children, of all races, were entitled to the same quality of education. This ruling was a major development in a growing civil rights movement: Blacks and other minorities were striving for full equality in all aspects of their lives, from freedom to ride in the front of a bus to freedom to drink from a water fountain marked "Whites Only." Many people, especially in the South, were reluctant to give up the old days of segregation. Tensions were high, and there was a strong danger of racial violence.

The Texas Rangers helped keep this period of change peaceful in Texas. Rangers got national attention in situations where their low-key but stern presence on school campuses prevented violent outbreaks. An ugly scene at the high school in the Tarrant County community of Mansfield was soon calmed when Rangers were called in. A photograph of Ranger Jay Banks leaning reflectively against a tree outside the high school as students went to class ran in newspapers and magazines all over the country.

Though dealing with integration troubles was a new duty for the Rangers, they faced that and their other duties in ways that upheld their old traditions.

When a riot broke out at the Rusk Hospital for the Criminally Insane and inmates took hostages, Ranger Capt. R. A. "Bob" Crowder walked alone into the maximum security unit. The Ranger captain and the leader of the mob had a little talk and the inmates surrendered. No one was hurt. Crowder's quiet courage convinced the prisoners they did not want to face the Texas Rangers.

Rangers also restored peace after a steel mill strike in East Texas became violent.

Another problem confronting the Rangers in the 1950s was illegal gambling.

* * * * *

J. J. Stewart stared out the classroom window at the waving palm tree. He was sitting in Texas history class, sixth period, but his mind was out on the bay, where the trout were supposed to be biting. As soon as school was out, he and his dad were going fishing.

Mrs. Bain's voice droned on like a passing shrimp boat — something you heard in the distance but tuned out.

"J. J., did you hear what I just said? I think you're daydreaming! J. J.!"

The giggling of the other kids snapped J. J. back into the present.

"I'm sorry, Mrs. Bain. I guess I missed what you said."

The other kids laughed again.

"I was explaining our term project," Mrs. Bain said. "Everyone is to find some interesting older person to talk to about their early memories of Galveston. You can use a tape recorder if you have one, or take notes on what they say. Then I want you to write a report on their recollections. I think you'll find there's a lot more to learn about history than what you can get out of a textbook."

J. J. and several of his classmates groaned.

"Mrs. Bain, that sounds too hard," Carl Shirley whined. "How do we know who to talk to? What do we ask them?"

J. J. was wondering the same thing, only he didn't want to say it out loud like Carl.

"Your homework assignment for this weekend is to think about who you might talk to," Mrs. Bain said. "Monday we'll go over all the possibilities. If you don't come up with something, I'll assign you someone to talk to."

J. J. wasn't a bad student, but he sure did like to fish. He was beginning to think about how fun it would be to fight a big redfish when the bell finally rang.

*   *   *   *   *

J. J. held his Houston Astros cap tightly by the brim as the flat-bottomed bay skimmer flew across the saltwater. There wasn't much wind, but the 125-horsepower outboard pushed the boat so fast even the small waves made for a teeth-rattling ride.

He and his dad had worked several of the good holes, catching two speckled trout, one keeper redfish, and a nice flounder.

The boat slowed and J. J. eased his grip on the Astros cap.

"Let's anchor off the old concrete ship and see if there are any more hungry redfish around," Bill Stewart said. "When I say 'drop it' let go the anchor, okay?"

J. J.'s dad let the boat drift a few more seconds.

"Okay, drop it!"

J. J. heaved the anchor off the bow. The boat still had enough momentum to keep drifting toward the old wreck, all that was left of an experimental freighter built of concrete during World War I. Suddenly, the anchor caught and the boat jerked and swung around as the line went taut.

"Now, let's see if there's some fish down there that want shrimp for dinner," his dad said, reaching into the ice chest that held the bait.

Father and son cast their lines toward the concrete wreck.

"There he is!" Bill Stewart yelled, jerking his rod back to set the hook. "Feels like a big bull red!"

J. J. watched his dad's rod bend into an upside-down U.

Then something tried to jerk J. J.'s rod from his hands.

"Dad, I got one too!"

*　　*　　*　　*　　*

The sun was getting low, painting the bay orange.

"Well, J. J., I guess we'd better leave a few fish for next time. Get the anchor up and let's go see if Mom wants to cook fish tonight."

J. J. put his rod in its holder, grabbed the anchor line, and gave it a tug. Nothing happened. J. J. pulled harder.

"It feels like its hung on something, Dad. I can't budge it!"

"Here, let me try it. Dang, we're anchored all right. Here, pull with me."

The two tugged as hard as they could. J. J. almost went over backward when the anchor finally came loose.

"I think we've 'caught' something else, J. J. Our anchor's coming up, but it feels like we're bringing something with it."

A rusty piece of metal broke out of the water.

"Well, I'll be darned," Bill Stewart said.

A crumpled box about the size of a TV set glistened on the deck of their boat. Three small square holes were arranged one next to the other on the front, a metal rod stuck out from one side.

"What is it, Dad?"

"It's an old one-armed bandit."

"What's that?"

"A slot machine. You stick in a coin, pull the lever, and watch the three windows. Three wheels with drawings on them roll inside, and if all three wheels match up, you win the jackpot. Trouble is, these things were designed to keep more money than they gave out. It was a sucker's game, J. J."

"Well, how did it end up in the bay?"

"The Texas Rangers put it there."

*   *   *   *   *

Three days later, J. J.'s dad dropped him off at an old house on Avenue O. Like most of the houses in the older part of Galveston, it had storm shutters and was built up on piers to protect it from hurricane flood waters.

"Just give me a call when ya'll are through talking," his dad said. "And don't forget to turn on your tape recorder."

Through his dad's friend, who was a reporter for the *Galveston News,* J. J. had come up with the person to talk to for his Texas history project: R. G. Birch, retired Texas Ranger. "R. G. can tell you all you need to know about how they got gambling out of Galveston," the reporter had told him.

J. J. knocked on the door.

"Hold your horses, I'm coming," a voice came from inside. Then a big hand pushed open the screen door.

"I expect you're J. J. Stewart. Come on in."

R. G. Birch still looked like a Texas Ranger, even though he was retired. He was so tall he had to stoop down a little to shake J. J.'s hand. He did not have a gun on, of course, but he wore a fancy leather belt and alligator hide boots.

"I hope you can help me with my Texas history project," J. J. started. "My dad and I were out fishing when we pulled an old slot machine out of the bay. Dad says the Texas Rangers put them there. I want to do my paper on what happened."

Birch laughed. "If you could see underwater, that whole bay bottom would look like it was covered with 'em. We tossed thousands of them in the water," he said.

"How come?" J. J. asked, turning on his tape recorder.

The former Ranger laughed again. "They don't call slot machines one-armed bandits for nothing," Birch began, settling back into a well-worn easy chair. "Sure, every once in a while some lucky fellow would hit a jackpot and money would come pouring out of one like a gumball machine gone crazy, but they were rigged so they didn't do that very often. Mostly they just took your money and didn't give anything back but the urge to put more money in and try your luck again."

"But how come you put the machines in the bay? Why didn't you make the people that had them get rid of them?" J. J. asked.

"The only way to keep those slots from being used again to rob somebody else was to destroy them," Birch said. "The folks that ran those gambling joints had plenty of money and political connections. They would have been open again the next day if we hadn't tossed all their gambling equipment — slot machines, roulette wheels, what have you — into the bay."

J. J. thought for a second. "Well, if having all that stuff was illegal, how come they were doing it? Was there some special reason they were doing it in Galveston?"

That made Birch pause for a moment.

"It seems funny now, all these years later, but back then, from the late thirties up to 1957, a lot of folks around here seemed to have the big idea that Galveston wasn't really a part of the rest of Texas. Maybe they figured that since Galveston is an island, all that water around it kept the law from coming across."

"Why didn't the Rangers do something when the gambling places first opened up?" J. J. asked.

"We did," Birch said. "I can't begin to tell you how many doors I've kicked in on this old island. We'd raid a joint one day and it would be open again the next night. Maybe two nights later, if we did a good job of collecting evidence. Problem was, there was no local prosecution. The district attorney's office and even some of the judges just didn't think closing gambling was very important. Gambling made Galveston a lot of money."

"So how did ya'll finally get rid of the gambling places?"

"Well, in 1956, a fellow named Will Wilson ran for state attorney general. He was a former prosecutor from Dallas and he made a campaign promise that if he was elected, he'd shut down illegal gambling in Galveston and anywhere else he found it. His idea was, and I agree with it, that wherever you have gambling, you've got problems with all kinds of crime — drugs, hijackings (that's what we used to call robberies), things like that."

Birch stood up.

"Why don't you turn that thing off for a while and I'll take you for a ride around town? I'll show you where some of the things we're talking about went on."

*   *   *   *   *

In a few minutes, J. J. and Birch were headed east on Seawall Boulevard.

"A lot of the joints used to be out there in the Gulf where you see those piers sticking out of the surf," Birch began. "The places looked like shoeboxes laid out from the seawall on top of those piers. The only way in was through the front door. There wasn't a back door, unless you wanted to get your feet wet."

Birch and J. J. both chuckled at that.

"Did some of those shell shops used to be gambling places?" J. J. asked.

"No, Hurricane Carla blew away the old joints," Birch said. "I think all these were built after 1961."

Birch pulled out of traffic on the Gulf side of the boulevard.

"Right about here was the old Balinese Room, probably the best known of all the gambling houses," he said. "It was a pretty fancy place. Fine food, dancing, famous entertainers like Frank Sinatra. The gambling went on out in the far back rooms. The only way to get to them was through a series of long, narrow hallways. By the time a Ranger could get to the back, all the gambling material would be hidden."

"If they were so good at hiding what they were doing, how did they get shut down?" J. J. asked.

"The Rangers, working with the Attorney General's Office, started planning a big raid on all the gambling places," Birch said, his car still idling next to the seawall sidewalk. "But we needed some evidence first, though everyone knew open gambling was going on. It was useless for a Ranger to try to get inside those places with his badge and guns on. So we brought in men who weren't known around here and sent them in, pretending to be tourists. They even took their wives in with 'em to make it look better. Well, we got enough evidence of gambling that way."

"So then what happened?"

"Colonel Homer Garrison, he was director of the Department of Public Safety back then, ordered sixty Rangers to meet up in Houston for a big raid on Galveston. We met in an auditorium there. You should have seen it. We had Rangers in from all over Texas — old boys who hadn't been out of the brush country for years. The attorney general had a bunch of men there, as well as the Liquor Control Board.

"We had some scouts down in Galveston watching the places. Not long before we were going to leave, Colonel Garrison got a telephone call. All the gambling places in Galveston — every one of them — had voluntarily shut down! Somebody had leaked them the word they were going to be raided. We never found out who did it."

"If you didn't raid all those places, how did the slot machines end up in the bay?"

"I'll get to that in a minute. Even though the big raid had to be called off, Colonel Garrison and Mr. Wilson figured the gambling folks intended to lay low for a while and then open back up once all the publicity had died down. But Mr. Wilson's men went to court and, using the information the Rangers and some of his investigators had come up with, got injunctions against about fifty gambling places . . . I know what you're going to ask next. An injunction is an order from a judge saying not to do something anymore."

"So what about the slot machines?" J. J. asked.

"The court orders stuck. We padlocked the joints and started collecting slot machines and about every other kind of gambling equipment you could think of. We burned a lot of the older wooden slot machines we found, but the metal ones we had to take sledge hammers to. After we'd banged them up enough so they couldn't be fixed, we took 'em out in the bay on barges and dumped 'em in."

By now they were at the end of the long boulevard. The pavement ended where the army had had a coastal artillery fort until the end of World War II. Across from there, on Bolivar Point, had been another post, Fort Travis, a collection of concrete gun emplacements and bunkers. Birch and J. J. got out of his car and stood in one of the old gun pits for a while, staring across the blue waters of the bay. A big oil tanker slid by on its way to Houston.

"A bunch of us Rangers spent the next several months tying up all the loose ends," Birch said. "A few of the gamblers weren't smart enough to see the writing on the wall. Gambling was finished on Galveston Island,

103

but some operators tried to stay open. We raided those places, and within three months, a long list of folks had been indicted for gambling."

Birch pointed across the bay where the other old fort was.

"Somebody hid three hundred slot machines in one of the underground bunkers over yonder," Birch said. "We got a tip that the machines were there and had us a little smash-up party. We let some of the reporters help us take the sledgehammer to those mechanical bandits. That's how I met your dad's friend on the paper. Anyhow, I think everybody had a pretty good time, except the gamblers when they found out about it."

*   *   *   *   *

Mrs. Bain finished marking the attendance numbers in her gradebook and looked up at the class.

"I want you to know I'm very pleased with your papers. I think I learned a thing or two myself about our city in reading all your reports. I don't want to embarrass anyone, but one person in class made an A-plus on his paper."

J. J. grinned. Maybe his dad would take him fishing again pretty soon.

10

The Missing
Dinosaur Tracks

The Texas Rangers are still serving the people of Texas, more than 165 years after Stephen F. Austin organized the first "ranging" company to protect his fledgling colony of settlers from Indians.

Many of the Ranger traditions have continued through the years, but today's Texas Ranger is more likely to jump into a helicopter than onto the back of a horse. Many Rangers still own their own horses, though, and sometimes use them to get places too rough for cars or even four-wheel-drive vehicles.

In 1991, the Rangers were made up of ninety-six men divided into six companies, "A" through "F." The elite group of lawmen are commanded by a senior Ranger captain and an assistant commander, who also is a captain. Six field captains, one for each company, report to these two men, who are stationed at the Department of Public Safety Headquarters in Austin. Each company captain has one sergeant and twelve to fifteen Rangers under him.

Today's Texas Rangers concentrate on major felony

crimes: murders, rapes, armed robbery, thefts. Rangers assist other police agencies in tracking down fugitives, and they work with the other services of the DPS, including Narcotics, Criminal Intelligence, and Motor Vehicle Theft. They also are increasingly involved in investigations of so-called "white collar crime" — cases involving complicated frauds and political corruption. In the rural areas of Texas, Rangers work closely with the Texas and Southwestern Cattle Raisers Association in handling cattle theft cases. Rangers also are called on to assist in restoring order in cases of civil unrest.

A Texas Ranger can enforce any law, anywhere in the state. Unlike city or county officers, a Ranger's authority does not end at the city limit sign or the county line. That is why Rangers are able to be of so much assistance to local agencies.

Most of a Ranger's time is spent investigating murders and robberies, but today's Ranger knows he is likely to run up on just about anything sooner or later, like tracking down rustlers — not cattle rustlers this time, but dinosaur footprint rustlers.

*   *   *   *   *

A pickup truck with no headlights on moved slowly down the bumpy, two-rut ranch road toward Fossil Creek. Three startled doe ran for the brush, their small hooves making clicking sounds on the limestone creekbed.

At first, Bob did not know why he was awake. He and Randy had horsed around inside their tent for an hour or two after midnight, playing tricks on each other, telling ghost stories, and talking about what they would do in the morning before sleep finally caught up with them. Now Bob was wide awake.

"Hey, Randy, wake up! I hear a pickup coming."

Randy did not come to instantly like Bob always did.

"It's just Granddad checking up on us again," a muffled voice said from somewhere inside the blue sleeping bag. "He'll leave when he sees our fire's out and we don't have our flashlights on in the tent. Go back to sleep so I can."

But Bob was already out of his sleeping bag, unzipping a slit in the tent flap to look out. The full moon was bright enough to make shadows. They had made their camp on the bluff over the creek so they could look down on it and most of the rest of the Broken Flint Ranch.

"It's not your granddad's pickup," Bob said. "There's no dog cage in the back."

At that, Randy crawled out of his bag.

"Mom and Dad went to Dallas and Ramundo took some heifers to Lockhart," Randy said. "Granddad's the only one on the whole ranch except us."

As the boys watched, two men got out of the truck. The driver tossed something and they heard a clank on the limestone.

"You wanna wake up ever'body in the county?" the passenger asked.

"There ain't nobody in twenty miles of here that can hear," the driver said. "I saw that old fool's pickup back at the ranch house, but this time of the morning, he's out like a light. Besides, he can't hear it thunder. Let's quit talking and get to work."

Randy grabbed his BB gun and cocked it.

"They're trespassing on our ranch. I'm going to tell 'em to get out of here," Randy said.

"*Shhhh,*" Bob whispered. "Are you crazy? Those guys would beat us up. I bet they're poachers. They'll have rifles. They aren't going to be scared of a BB gun."

"Okay, maybe you're right. But what are we going to do? This ranch is posted — no trespassing allowed."

"There's not much we can do but watch and see what happens," Bob whispered. "I'm just glad we're up here in the brush where they can't see our tent. Let's don't let them hear us."

The two men moved down into the creek. Two flashlight beams played back and forth over the wide limestone. Once, a light hit the tent, but it did not linger.

"Here they are," one of the men said.

"Okay, now what?" his partner asked.

"Just hold the light for me."

A gasoline motor exploded to life, the roar echoing down the creek.

"That's a power saw," Bob said. "What are they going to cut up out there in the creekbed?"

Randy was about to say he had no idea when it hit him suddenly and solidly.

"Oh, my gosh! They're stealing the dinosaur tracks!"

The masonry saw screamed as it cut into the ancient limestone.

*   *   *   *   *

Texas Ranger Luis Garcia had always been an early riser. He liked to get up, drink plenty of coffee, and read the morning paper. As he pulled his unmarked car out of his driveway, he picked up his radio microphone.

"Six nine nine — Austin," he said, calling the Department of Public Safety's district office.

"Austin — six nine nine," the dispatcher's voice replied.

"I'll be ten–eight, en route to the shops," Rogers said.

"Ten–four, six nine nine. Be advised Sheriff Risinger wants you to call him as soon as possible."

As the mechanic filled the Ranger's car with gas, Garcia dialed the sheriff's office in nearby Hays County.

"I've got a strange one I thought you'd like to hear about," the sheriff said. "We've got some rustlers on our hands."

"Who lost cattle this time?" Garcia asked, fishing for his pen.

"Not cattle, Luis," the sheriff said. "Dinosaurs. Dinosaur tracks, leastwise. Couple of fellows slipped out to the Broken Flint Ranch last night and used a stone saw to cut a block of dinosaur tracks right out of the creek bed. Nothing where that old dinosaur squished his toes in the mud but a smooth, square hole. Owner doesn't know how much the tracks would be worth, but I imagine it's a felony theft. Criminal mischief if nothing else. Can you meet me out there and take a look?"

"I'm on my way, J. W.," Garcia said.

*   *   *   *   *

Bob and Randy and Randy's grandfather, Bill Mc-Neil, were still down in the creek when the Rangers and the sheriff pulled up in their cars. A deputy stood with them.

Bob watched as the Ranger unlimbered himself from his car.

Luis Garcia was a big man, but he moved gracefully. He wore tan jeans, a starchy white Western-style shirt, and a straw summer cowboy hat. But what caught Bob's eye was the big, silver pistol in the hand-tooled leather holster on his narrow hip and the bright round badge — a five-point star in a circle — pinned on his chest.

"I just can't figure it," McNeil said after shaking hands with the two officers and introducing them to Bob and Randy. "I know there's folks who'll steal anything that isn't nailed down, but I never thought anybody would carry off my dinosaur tracks. You know, it's not every ranch that has a creek that a dinosaur walked up. I don't like trespassers and I don't like this one darn bit. They're not making dinosaurs anymore! Now, I'm just fresh out of tracks."

The Ranger listened quietly as Randy's granddad went on about trespassers and dinosaur track rustlers.

"The sheriff tells me you boys saw some people out here last night," Garcia said, turning to Bob and Randy. "Tell me about it."

"They've already told everything to the deputy," Grandpa McNeil said. "You're a Ranger, go find them thieves before I get my .30-.30 and go after them myself."

109

"We'll do the best we can, Mr. McNeil, but I need a little more to go on than a square hole in a creekbed," Garcia said patiently.

Bob and Randy told the Ranger what they had seen.

"Can either of you boys describe those fellows?" the Ranger asked.

"Well, the moon was pretty bright," Bob said. "One man was kind of fat, the other was short and thin. I could tell they had a hard time getting the rock up on the pickup. They didn't talk very nice."

The Ranger kneeled down and looked at the hole where the tracks had been. "They used a couple of crowbars to pry the stone out once they finished cutting around the tracks," he said. "Here are the pry marks in the limestone. Can't tell anything about what kind of shoes they had on since this is solid rock, but if they were locals, I expect they were wearing boots. And they must be from around here, or they wouldn't know about the tracks. Have you had any strangers asking to see the tracks, Mr. McNeil?"

"Nope, nobody's been around the place all summer. But like you say, everybody around here knows I've got the tracks. They're the only dinosaur tracks between here and the state park up at Glen Rose."

Ranger Garcia stood and pushed his hat back a little.

"Boys, can you show me where they parked their pickup?"

Bob and Randy led the Ranger to the spot where the truck had stopped, just short of the low water crossing across the creek.

"I think they were drinking beer," Bob said. "One of them tossed a can. I heard it hit a rock."

The Ranger kicked around the grass for a second before exposing a beer can.

Randy stooped to pick it up.

"Don't touch it, son," the Ranger said. "Dry as it's been, I expect the lab people will be able to get some fingerprints off that can. If not the can, this."

The Ranger held up a paper sack. Inside were two other empty beer cans and a cardboard container that once held a six-pack.

"I expect they left their truck here until they got the tracks cut loose, then they came back and drove over to the spot so they could load up the stone," the Ranger said.

The Ranger, the sheriff, and his deputy walked around in the dry grass between the road leading down into the creekbed and a barbed wire fence.

"One of the men must have walked over toward the fence a piece," the Ranger said. "Here are some boot tracks. He's either got a bad leg or a mighty poor old pair of boots, because he's leaving a deeper heel print on one side than the other."

The Ranger kneeled to pick something up.

"He must have finished his last cigarette while he was standing here. Here's the butt and here's his crumpled-up pack. Doesn't look like they've been on the ground long, but I guess anybody could have tossed 'em here."

"No, it must have been the thieves," Grandpa McNeil said. "We've got a strict rule on this place. Your trash goes in the back of the pickup, not on the ground. Besides, I don't know anybody who comes on this place who smokes."

The Ranger walked over to his car, opened the trunk, and dug around inside for some plastic bags to put the evidence in.

"I'll take this stuff to the lab and see what they can come up with."

"Are you going to go get your horse now and track 'em down?" Randy asked.

"No, son, the Rangers don't do much riding these days. I spend more time up in a helicopter than I do on the back of a horse, but I still have one, just in case."

"Neat! You get to ride in helicopters? Can Bob and I go up with you sometime?"

"Well, son, I expect the colonel wouldn't want our tax

111

dollars spent taking a boy up in a helicopter, but stranger things have happened," the Ranger said. "Right now we've got to concentrate on these missing tracks."

The Ranger and Sheriff Risinger started walking back toward their cars. The deputy, Bob, Randy, and Grandpa McNeil followed.

"Boys, did ya'll get a good enough look at that pickup to recognize it if you saw it again?" the Ranger asked.

"I think I did," Bob said. "I saw it first and I remember it had pipes laying on a rack over the bed."

"You didn't write down the license plate number, did you?"

"No, sir. It was too dark, but I thought about it. I just couldn't see the numbers from where we were or I would have," Bob said.

The Ranger smiled. "I guess that would have made it too easy. How would you boys like to make a little run with me? That okay with you, Mr. McNeil?"

Bob rode in the front seat, Randy in the back.

The Ranger reached for his radio microphone. "I'd better check and see if anything else is going on. I've got several other cases I'm waiting for some calls on."

A small red light on the radio beneath the dash flashed on when the Ranger keyed the microphone.

"Six nine nine — Austin. I'll be en route to Cedar Springs. Any traffic?"

"Negative, six nine nine. No calls," the communications operator replied.

"Six nine nine — Austin. I'm looking for a blue over white or green over white pickup truck with a pipe rack over the bed. Probably will still be in Hays County and it could be riding a little low in the back. No other description and no license number."

"Ten-four, six nine nine. Do you want it to go out to all regions?"

"Negative, Austin. Just this area."

The Ranger turned to Bob. "If I'm right, those men

haven't gone far. I expect they think no one is going to miss those dinosaur tracks for a while."

It did not take long to cover the town. They looked at a lot of pickup trucks, but none that the boys could positively say was the one they had seen the night before.

"Well, let's try something else," the Ranger said. "Unless they happen to be in the masonry trade, they had to get that saw somewhere. Let's see what Jack Fentress has been renting lately."

The Ranger pulled his car up in front of "If We Don't Have It, It's Not For Rent," Cedar Springs' only rental service.

"Hi, Jack. We could use a little help. Have you rented anyone a masonry saw lately?"

Fentress reached below the counter for his receipt book.

"That's not my most popular item," Fentress said. "It stays there in the back most of the time. Let's see. Yep, rented it day before yesterday. Why you interested, Luis?"

The Ranger pulled out the notebook he carried in a handtooled leather cover that matched his holster.

"Well, it may not mean a thing, but I'm looking for somebody who carried off Bill McNeil's dinosaur tracks. Whoever did it used a masonry saw."

Fentress handed Garcia the rental agreement.

"I'm glad you got his driver license number, Jack. That'll sure make things easier. And Jack, I'd appreciate it if you kept this confidential. This old boy may not be our man at all, and I wouldn't want his family to be embarrassed. I'd also appreciate it if you'd just keep it in the back for a while. I may be sending somebody from the lab by to check it for prints."

Back in his car, Garcia picked up his radio microphone.

"Six nine nine — Austin. Need a 27 and 29 on Texas DL 5839373. Give me a 43 too."

"Ten—four, six nine nine."

113

"What all are you asking for?" Bob asked.

"Well, I want to make sure the fellow who rented that saw is who he says he is. They'll check the computers to see if that's his real name and whether we have any arrest warrants for him. The 43, that's a criminal history. Tells whether he's ever been arrested and what for."

"Why do you need to know all that stuff?" Randy asked.

"You boys ask more questions than reporters," Garcia said. "Most of the people who break the law have broken it before. That's one reason. Another is I just like to cover every base."

"Austin — six nine nine. Texas DL, issued to Rick Rhodes, 4907 Bosque Street, Cedar Springs. One citation for speeding. No 29. Criminal history negative."

Garcia wrote down the name. "Well, if he's our man, he's never done anything worse than drive too fast."

"Maybe he just hasn't gotten caught for anything yet," Randy offered.

*   *   *   *   *

The Ranger drove by the address given for Rhodes. When he saw no one was home, he headed back to the ranch.

After taking photographs of the hole left in the creekbed by the thieves, Garcia left for Austin to hand the evidence over to the crime laboratory.

Before leaving, he gave both boys his business card.

"If you two see that pickup truck around town, give me a call. I've got some other cases to work on until he shows up. When he does, we'll go from there."

A week later, Garcia called Bill McNeil.

"Ranger from Company A down in Houston called me this morning with some pretty interesting information," Garcia said. "He didn't get the man's name, but somebody built about like the person who rented a masonry saw in Cedar Springs, and fitting the same description as one of the men the boys saw that night, came into his pawn shop on Telephone Road. Asked if he was interested in buying a set of dinosaur footprints. Manager told him no, said he didn't have much call for prehistoric tracks. Said he could sell all the VCRs he could get, though.

"Anyway, I've sent a copy of Rhodes' driver license picture to Houston. One of the Rangers is going to do what we call a photo line-up. He'll mix Rhodes' picture with several others. Then he'll show the pictures to the man at the pawn shop. If he picks Rhodes, we'll have something to go on."

*   *   *   *   *

Randy and Bob were plunking with their BB guns a few days later when they saw Ranger Garcia's brown car approaching the ranch house.

"Hi, boys. Your granddad around?"

Bob volunteered to go get him.

"Well, Ranger, have you found my dinosaur tracks?" Grandpa McNeil said as he greeted Garcia.

"No, Mr. McNeil, I haven't. But I believe we're making progress. Rick Rhodes, that fellow from Cedar Springs, has been positively identified as the man who tried to sell the tracks down in Houston."

"Then why don't you just go arrest him and get my tracks back?"

"I wish it was that easy, Mr. McNeil. I know it's hard for folks to swallow, but suspects and crooks have got the same rights you and I have. We've got to take it step by step.

"I've been doing some background work on him. He sells antiques and junk on the side. I've driven by his place a few times. If he's got your tracks, they're somewhere you can't see from the street. But the district attorney believes we've got enough probable cause for a search warrant. I just wanted to let you know we're going to be

115

paying him a little visit tomorrow before he leaves for work."

Randy and Bob had not been particularly interested in all the legal talk. But that changed when they heard Ranger Garcia say he planned to search the house.

"Can we go?" they shouted in unison.

The Ranger studied them for a second and grinned.

"Well, when you go busting into someone's house early in the morning with a piece of paper, some folks get a little overexcited. I can't take you in a state car this time, but if you two just happen to be fooling around on your bicycles, might not anybody notice.

"Of course, your granddad would have to give me his approval, and you would have to give me your word not to tell anybody what we're going to do. You'd have to stay out of the way, but I may be too busy to notice a couple of kids have wandered up to the house to see what all the commotion was about. You two can't go inside the house, though."

Randy and Bob went outside to practice kicking open the old woodshed door, just in case their skills might be needed in the morning.

Garcia waited until they were out of earshot.

"Those are good boys, Mr. McNeil. It's easy enough these days for a kid to head off in the wrong direction. I don't think we'll have any trouble tomorrow. If that old boy is our man, he's just a thief, and an amateur one at that. The boys won't be in any danger."

McNeil nodded. "I appreciate what you're doing, Luis. I'll appreciate it even more if you find my darn tracks."

*   *   *   *   *

If Randy and Bob had not known what was up, they probably would not have noticed anything unusual going on that morning. Ranger Garcia and two sheriff's cars pulled up outside the house at about 7:00.

One of the deputies slipped around to the back of the

116

house while Ranger Garcia and the other deputy went to the front door. The deputy knocked and, as the boys watched from across the street, someone opened the door and let them inside.

From room to room, all the lights in the house snapped on. Occasionally, the boys could see shadows moving from window to window.

"How long do you think it'll take?" Randy asked. "Seems like they've been in there a long time. Let's go over in front of the house and see if we can hear anything."

A fresh load of dirt covered a part of the yard on the edge of the driveway like a slightly melted scoop of chocolate ice cream sprinkled with crumpled Oreo cookies.

To pass the time, Randy picked up a dirt clod and threw it at Bob. Bob reached down and grabbed another clod to hurl back at Randy.

That's when Bob saw a flash of white in the dirt.

"Hey, look! There's a big rock under the dirt. It's got a square corner!"

The two boys dived into the dirt, sweeping soil off the rock.

"It's the tracks!" Bob said. "I guess he figured he could hide them here until he could find somebody who'd buy 'em. Must have heard the Rangers were after him."

"Let's go tell Luis," Randy said.

"We're not supposed to be playing in this man's dirt pile," Bob said. "If we say we found the tracks, it might mess up things and they couldn't put this guy in jail for stealing them."

Both boys jumped up when they heard the front door open. The Ranger stepped out on the porch with a pair of cowboy boots in his hand.

"I think these boot heels are going to match the tracks I found out there at the ranch," the Ranger told one of the deputies. "All we need is to find the tracks."

Bob whispered to Randy.

* * * * *

"Ouch!" Bob yelled, grabbing his knee. "It hurts!"

"What are you kids doing out this time of the morning?" one of the deputies asked.

The Ranger seemed about to say something when Bob began rolling on the ground, moaning in agony.

"We were just playing, officer," Randy told the deputy. "I was chasing Bob and he fell on the dirt and started hollering something had hurt his knee. We didn't mean to be any trouble."

Garcia walked over to the dirt pile and kneeled down next to Bob.

"I hit that big rock," Bob managed to say between groans.

The Ranger looked over at the partially exposed hunk of limestone and smiled. "Sure lucky you didn't cut yourself on that sharp corner," he said.

* * * * *

The boys were shooting tin cans off fence posts with their BB guns when they heard the whirring noise. A blue and gray helicopter looked like it was headed straight for the ranch house.

"It's going to land," Bob shouted.

The tall Ranger ducked low as he walked quickly from under the swirling rotors.

"Hello, boys. I just wanted you and Mr. McNeil to know that fellow plead guilty to stealing the tracks. The district attorney decided to drop the charges against his buddy. Doing the stealing was Rhodes' idea, anyway. The other guy was mostly just along for the ride," Garcia said.

Grandpa McNeil had heard the helicopter and had come outside to see what all the commotion was.

"Mr. McNeil, I bet the people at the museum there in Austin really appreciate your giving them the tracks.

But I doubt your tracks would have been found if it hadn't been for these boys. If it's all right with you, I thought we'd take 'em up in the helicopter for a while. Never know when we might need a couple extra sets of good eyes. I wouldn't be surprised if you boys aren't Rangers someday."

Glossary

adjutant — A staff officer who helps the commanding officer.

adjutant general — The chief administrative officer of a military unit; in Texas, until 1935, the commander of the Texas Rangers.

Anglo — Person of white or English heritage.

artillery — Cannons.

attorney general — Chief law officer of the state, who serves as legal advisor.

baile — (Spanish) A dance.

bantam — Small.

barbed wire — Twisted wire with sharp points, used as fencing.

battalion — A large military unit in the army.

blind — A hidden place that conceals a hunter or shooter.

bootlegger — Person who smuggles or sells alcoholic beverages illegally.

brace — A pair of similar things.

brake — Rough land overgrown with one kind of plant.

broadcloth — A fine, smooth woolen cloth.

buck — Male deer.

buckshot — Large, round pellets used in shotguns.

buckskin — Deer skin, or clothes made of deer skin.

burro — A donkey used as a pack animal.

cantina — (Spanish) A small barroom or saloon.

carbine — A light, short-barreled rifle.

cinch — Strap to fasten a saddle to a horse.

conchos — (Spanish) Silver ornaments.

contraband — Illegally imported or smuggled goods.

counterattack — A defensive or opposing attack made against the enemy.

cronies — Slang term for friends or associates.

culvert — A drain.

dead ringer — A duplicate; a person or animal that very closely resembles another person or animal.

doggedly — Persistently; stubbornly determined.

duck pants — Trousers made of light-colored, durable cotton or linen cloth.

dust devils — Small whirlwinds of sand or dust.

empresarios — (Spanish) Land agents or land contractors used by the Mexican government to bring colonists into Texas.

equipage — Supplies needed to outfit a group of riders or soldiers.

felonies — Major crimes, such as murders or robberies.

frijoles — (Spanish) Beans.

frock coat — A man's double-breasted, knee-length coat.

frontier — The edge of settlement.

fugitive — A person attempting to avoid capture.

gelding — A horse that has been castrated.

goatee — Small, pointed beard on a man's chin.

grub — Food.

guerrilla attacks — Harassments by irregular fighters.

gusher — Oil well with a plentiful flow.

Hispanic — Descendant of Spanish-speaking people.

hombres — (Spanish) Guys or fellows.

indicted — Accused or charged with a crime.

infantry — Foot soldier.

injunction — An order of the court to do or not to do something.

look-see — A general survey or investigation.

lynch mob — A large group acting without legal authority to injure or kill someone.

mesquite — Spiny tree that forms thickets in Mexico and the Southwest.

milch cow — A cow from which milk is taken.

muzzle-loader — A type of firearm that is loaded down its barrel.

nib — The point of a quill pen or ink pen.

norther — A cold, strong north wind that brings a sudden drop in temperature.

notorious — Widely but unfavorably known.

palavering — Discussing.

parleyed — Talked or discussed.

pick-ax — A heavy, wooden-handled digging tool pointed at both ends.

posse — A large group brought together by the sheriff or other legal authority in an emergency.

poultice — Material, such as herbs, pressed on a wound to heal it.

purse — The sum of money offered as a prize.

quarry — Game or prey.

quirt — A riding whip, often of braided leather.

railheads — Beginning or end of railroad line.

rampant — Widespread; uncontrolled.

resaca — (Spanish) Bodies of water created when a river changes course.

scabbard — Leather sheath for a rifle or carbine.

secession — The withdrawal of eleven Southern states from the Federal Union in 1860–61; the cause of the Civil War.

segregation — The separation of a race of people from the rest of society.

señorita — (Spanish) An unmarried girl.

six-shooter — A pistol with a revolving cylinder holding six bullets.

sombrero — (Spanish) Hat.

spiel — A line of extravagant talk; a sales pitch.

squaw — (Algonquin) An Indian; once used for any American-Indian woman.

teetotaler — A person who never drinks alcohol.

tequileros — Border Mexican term for those who smuggled liquor.

undercover — Spying or making a secret investigation.

veto — An order prohibiting a proposed or intended act.

victuals — Supplies of food; pronounced as "vittles."

voucher — A document or certificate exchanged for payment.

wagering — Betting or gambling.

More Books About the Texas Rangers

If you want to learn more about the history of the Texas Rangers, here are some books you should be able to find at your school or public library. Over the years, many good books have been written about the Rangers. Unfortunately, some of them are out of print and hard to find. The books listed here are all still available from their publisher.

Davis, John L. *The Texas Rangers: Their First 150 Years*. San Antonio: Institute of Texan Cultures, 1975.

Day, James M. *Captain Clint Peoples: Texas Ranger*. Waco: Texian Press, 1980.

Durham, George. *Taming the Nueces Strip: The Story of McNelly's Rangers*. Austin: University of Texas Press, 1962.

Gillett, James B. *Six Years With the Texas Rangers*. Lincoln: University of Nebraska Press, 1976.

Greer, James K. *Colonel Jack Hays: Texas Frontier Leader and California Builder*. College Station: Texas A&M Press, 1986.

Hughes, W. J. *Rebellious Ranger: Rip Ford and the Old Southwest*. Norman: University of Oklahoma Press, 1964.

Malsch, Brownson. *Captain M. T. Gonzaullas*. Austin: Shoal Creek Publishers, 1980.

Martin, Jack. *Border Boss: Captain John R. Hughes — Texas Ranger*. Austin: State House Press, 1990.

Paine, Albert Bigelow. *Captain Bill McDonald: Texas Ranger*. Austin: State House Press, 1985.

Procter, Ben. *Just One Riot*. Austin: Eakin Press, 1991.

Roberts, Dan. *Rangers and Sovereignty*. Austin: State House Press, 1987.

Sowell, A. J. *Life of "Big Foot" Wallace.* Austin: State House Press, 1989.

———. *Rangers and Pioneers of Texas.* Austin: State House Press, 1991.

Sterling, William W. *Trails and Trials of a Texas Ranger.* Norman: University of Oklahoma Press, 1968.

Webb, Walter P. *The Texas Rangers: A Century of Frontier Defense.* Austin: University of Texas Press, 1965.

Wilkins, Frederick. *The Highly Irregular Irregulars: Texas Rangers in the Mexican War.* Austin: Eakin Press, 1991.

Ranger Ron Stewart. Modern Texas Rangers still know how to shoot straight.
— Photo courtesy Texas Department of Public Safety

Captain John R. Hughes, the Lone Star Ranger.
— Photo by L. A. Wilke

Captain John Armstrong, Captain of State Rangers, and captor of John Wesley Hardin.

*Captain Leander H. McNelly, prominent old-time Texas
Ranger.*

Captain Jack Hays, copy of painting in the Alamo.
— Photo courtesy Western History Collection,
University of Oklahoma Library

*TEXAS RANGERS, AT TEMPLE, TEXAS, RAILROAD
STRIKE, JULY 1894. Left to right, standing: Capt. J. A.
Brooks, Co. F; Capt. J. R. Hughes, Co. D; Private John Nix,
Co. E; Corp. E. D. Aten, Co. D; Private Ed. Connell, Co. B;
Corp. T. M. Ross, Co. E; Private Lee Queen, Co. B; Private
A. A. Neeley, Co. B; Private G. J. Cook, Co. F; Private Dan
Coleman, Co. E. Sitting: Private Jack Harrell, Co. B; Private
Will Schmidt, Co. D; Private C. B. Fullerton, Co. B; Private
G. N. Horton, Co. F; Private Ed. Palmer, Co. D; Private Joe
Natus, Co. F; Private J. V. Latham, Co. D; Private E. E.
Coleman, Co. F.* — Photo courtesy Western History Collection,
University of Oklahoma Library

Rangers of the Frontier Battalion helped tame Texas.
— Photo from author's collection

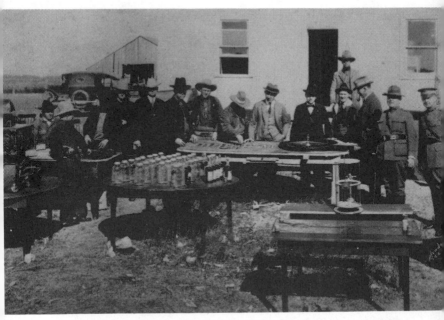

Rangers with confiscated bootleg whiskey and gambling equipment.
— Photo courtesy Texas Ranger Hall of Fame, Waco, Texas

Texas Rangers camp in 1887.
— Photo from author's collection

The riding done by most modern Texas Rangers is largely ceremonial.
— Photo by Mike Cox

Both the horse and the helicopter are used to track down criminals. The pilots shown here are Joe Herring (in helicopter) and Roy Sweatman (holding map). The Rangers are (from left) Capt. E. G. Albers (now retired), Joe Davis, and George Brakefield.

— Photo courtesy Texas Department of Public Safety

This Texas Ranger statue guards passengers at Dallas' Love Field.

— Photo by L. A. Wilke

Capt. Frank Hamer tracked down Bonnie and Clyde.
— Photo from author's collection

Bonnie and Clyde's car.
— Photo from author's collection